CHRISTIAN STUDIES IV

A Chronological Overview of the Bible

Teacher Guide

MEMORIA PRESS

TEACHING GUIDELINES

The goal of ***Christian Studies IV*** is to provide students with an overview of what is in the Bible - like a map that they can carry with them in their heads. This program will be most effective if students memorize the drill questions and have instant recall of the basic information that is in each book of the Bible. The knowledge that is placed in students' permanent memories is knowledge that they will carry with them throughout their lives.

- Complete the overview of each book of the Bible by discussing and having students complete the fill-in-the-blank section of each lesson. Answers are to be found in the *Christian Studies IV: A Chronological Overview of the Bible* text and/or the Scripture verses indicated in parentheses.
- Review the Scripture passages in the appendix that pertain to the lesson for the week. See how many your students remember from *Christian Studies I-III*. Encourage them to memorize as many as possible.
- Give students a set amount of time to complete the drill questions in the appendix. Your goal is to see how much they know about the Book they are studying. They should answer as many questions as possible that they have instant recall on. When time is up, they can use the Scripture passage reference next to the question for the answers they don't know. They can look up and read the stories they need to review. Then, they can complete the drill questions they didn't know.
- Students should be made responsible for learning the memory verse for each lesson in addition to the drill questions in the appendix. Begin your next class with a recitation of previously memorized Scripture verses as well as an oral review of the drill questions studied in previous lessons.

MEMORIA PRESS
www.MemoriaPress.com

CHRISTIAN STUDIES IV
A Chronological Overview of the Bible

TEACHER GUIDE
Contributing Editors: HLS Faculty

ISBN 978-1-61538-090-9

Cover illustration by Masaccio

TABLE OF CONTENTS

Contains all of the Scripture verses and drill questions from Memoria Press' *Christian Studies I - III.*

BIBLE

The Bible is a collection of 66 books divided into two major sections. The first section is called the Old Testament and provides a historical account of the people of Israel from Creation to the return of the exiles to Palestine. The second section is called the New Testament and begins with the birth of Jesus and continues through to the establishment of the first century Church.

1. Number of books in the Old Testament: Orthodox: 49*; Protestant: 39; Catholic: 46
2. Number of books in the New Testament: 27
3. Another word for "testament" is covenant.

*Orthodox Christians vary in the number of books they include, but students are only required to know/supply "49" in this guide.

A **covenant** is an arrangement made between two people. The Bible provides the basis for how man is to interact with God and what is required of him by God. The Bible was given by God to man for his spiritual guidance and benefit.

The Bible has many contributing authors but is wholly the Word of God. The concept that what was written in the Bible was completely directed and guided by God is called the doctrine of inspiration.

Some traditions include a section of historical books called the deuterocanonical books. These writings are found in a Greek translation of the Hebrew Scriptures called the Septuagint, but not in the Hebrew canon. These include both full books and additional sections within books found in the Hebrew canon.

OLD TESTAMENT

Jewish tradition refers to the Old Testament books as the ___Tanak___. This word is an acronym formed from the three sections that comprise the Jewish scriptures (or Masoretic Text). These three sections are:

1. The Law: ___Torah___
2. The Prophets: ___Neviim___
3. The Writings: ___Ketuvim___

THE PENTATEUCH

The first five books of the Old Testament are called the Pentateuch. The term was formed by two Greek words, *pente* which means "five" and *teuchos* which means "book." This "five volume book" was called the Torah by the Jews and is referred to throughout the Scriptures as the ___Book of Moses___ or ___the Law___.

The books of the Pentateuch:

A. ___Genesis___

B. ___Exodus___

C. ___Leviticus___

D. ___Numbers___

E. ___Deuteronomy___

The author of the Pentateuch was ___Moses___.

The time period covered within the Pentateuch: ___Creation- Arrival at Canaan in c. 1400 B.C.___

OLD TESTAMENT

LAW
Genesis
Exodus
Leviticus
Numbers
Deuteronomy

HISTORY
Joshua
Judges
Ruth
I II Samuel
I II Kings
I II Chronicles
Ezra
Nehemiah
Esther

WISDOM
Job
Psalms
Proverbs
Ecclesiastes
Song of Solomon

MAJOR PROPHETS
Isaiah
Jeremiah
Lamentations
Ezekiel
Daniel

MINOR PROPHETS
Hosea
Joel
Amos
Obadiah
Jonah
Micah
Nahum
Habakkuk
Zephaniah
Haggai
Zechariah
Malachi

DEUTEROCANON (when included)
Tobit
Judith
1 Maccabees
2 Maccabees
Wisdom
Sirach
Baruch

*Books of the Bible in canonical order

GENESIS

Key People:

1. The first human beings: Adam and Eve
2. The man whom God used to preserve mankind during the flood: Noah
3. The Patriarchs: Abraham, Isaac, and Jacob
4. The man whom God used to preserve Israel during the famine in Egypt: Joseph

Key Terms:

creatio ex nihilo: creation out of nothing

imago Dei: image of God

patriarch: head of a tribe or family; founder of a group

covenant: a binding agreement between two parties

Outline:

1. God created the world in 6 days. (Gen. 1:1-2:25)
2. Because man disobeyed God, sin entered the world. This event is called the Fall. (Gen.3)
3. Man became wicked and God punished the earth with a flood. (Gen. 6:5-8, 13-18; 8:20-22)
4. God confused the language of man at the Tower of Babel. (Gen. 11:1-9)
5. Abram is called and God makes a covenant with him to make him a great nation and bless all nations through him in 2000 B.C.. (Gen. 12:1-9)
6. God promised Abraham and his descendants the land of Canaan. (Gen. 12:1-9)
7. God destroys the two wicked cities of Sodom and Gomorrah. (Gen. 18:20-21: 19:23-29)
8. God asks Abraham to sacrifice his son Isaac, but provides a ram for the sacrifice. (Gen. 22:9-14)
9. Jacob wrestles with God and is given the name Israel. (Gen. 32:24-31)
10. God uses Joseph to preserve the Israelites during famine, and Genesis ends with the Israelites in Egypt. (Gen. 50:15-26)

Memory Verses:

Genesis 1:26-28

And God said, Let us make man in our image, after our likeness; and let them have dominion over the fish of the sea, and over the fowl of the air, and over the cattle, and over all the earth. So God created man in his own image, in the image of God created he him; male and female created he them. And God blessed them, and God said unto them, Be fruitful, and multiply, and replenish the earth, and subdue it.

Genesis 12:1-3 (The Call of Abraham)

Now the Lord said unto Abram, Get thee out of thy country and from thy kindred and from thy father's house, unto a land that I will show thee; And I will make of thee a great nation and I will bless thee, and in thee shall all families of the earth be blessed.

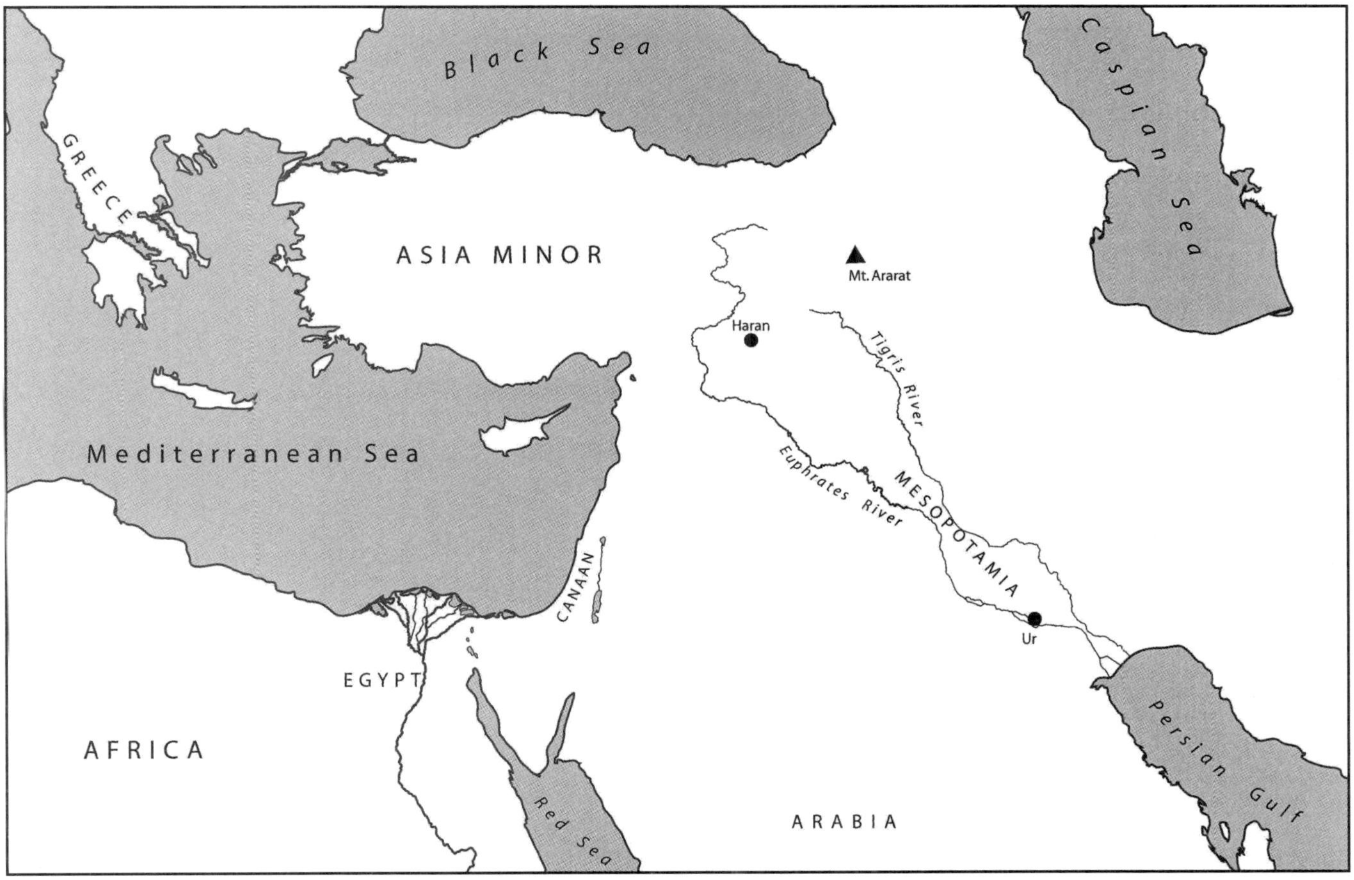

EXODUS

Key People:

1. The man who led Israel out of bondage in Egypt: Moses
2. The man who spoke for Moses and was the first High Priest of Israel: Aaron
3. The man who defied God and refused to free the people of Israel: Pharaoh

Key Terms:

redemption: rescue, deliverance

Passover: Jewish celebration of God's deliverance of Israel from bondage

promised land: the land promised by God to the descendants of Abraham; Canaan

tabernacle: tent, center of worship for the Hebrews

Outline:

1. The people of Israel are put in bondage and God calls Moses through a burning bush to deliver them. (Exodus 3:1-22)
2. Pharaoh refuses to free the Israelites and God sends 10 plagues to punish the Egyptians. (Exodus 7-12)

The Ten Plagues	
1. Water in Egypt turned to blood (7:20)	6. Boils (9:10)
2. Frogs (8:6)	7. Hail (9:23)
3. Gnats (8:17)	8. Locusts (10:13)
4. Flies (8:24)	9. Darkness (10:22)
5. Livestock died (9:6)	10. Death of firstborn (12:29)

3. Israelites observe the first Passover, during which God spared the firstborn sons of Israel. (Ex. 12:21-28, 43-49)
4. Israel escapes the army of Pharaoh because God parts the Red Sea in 1400 B.C.. (Ex. 14:21-25)
5. God gives Moses the Ten Commandments at Mount Sinai. (Ex. 20:1-21)

The Ten Commandments	
Catholic/Lutheran	Protestant
1. I am the Lord your God: you shall have no gods before me. 2. You shall not take the name of the Lord your God in vain. 3. Remember the Sabbath and keep it holy. 4. Honor thy father and mother. 5. Thou shall not kill. 6. Thou shall not commit adultery. 7. Thou shall not steal. 8. Thou shall not bear false witness against your neighbor. 9. Thou shall not covet your neighbor's wife. 10. Thou shall not covet your neighbor's goods.	1. I am the Lord your God: you shall have no gods before me. 2. You shall not make any graven images. 3. You shall not take the name of the Lord your God in vain. 4. Remember the Sabbath and keep it holy. 5. Honor thy father and mother. 6. You shall not kill. 7. You shall not commit adultery. 8. You shall not steal. 9. You shall not bear false witness against your neighbor. 10. You shall not covet thy neighbor's house nor his wife nor anything that belongs to him.

6. The people are punished for idolatrous worship when they had Aaron make for them a

 golden calf . (Ex. 32:1-9)

7. According to God's command, the Israelites built the Tabernacle

 and the Ark of the Covenant . (Ex. 40:16-21)

Memory Verse:

Exodus 3:13-14

And Moses said unto God, Behold, when I come unto the children of Israel and shall say unto them, The God of your fathers has sent me unto you and they shall say unto me, What is his name? What shall I say unto them? And God said unto Moses, I AM THAT I AM; and he said, Thus shalt you say unto the children of Israel, I AM hath sent me unto you.

*Memorize the Ten Commandments

THE EXODUS:

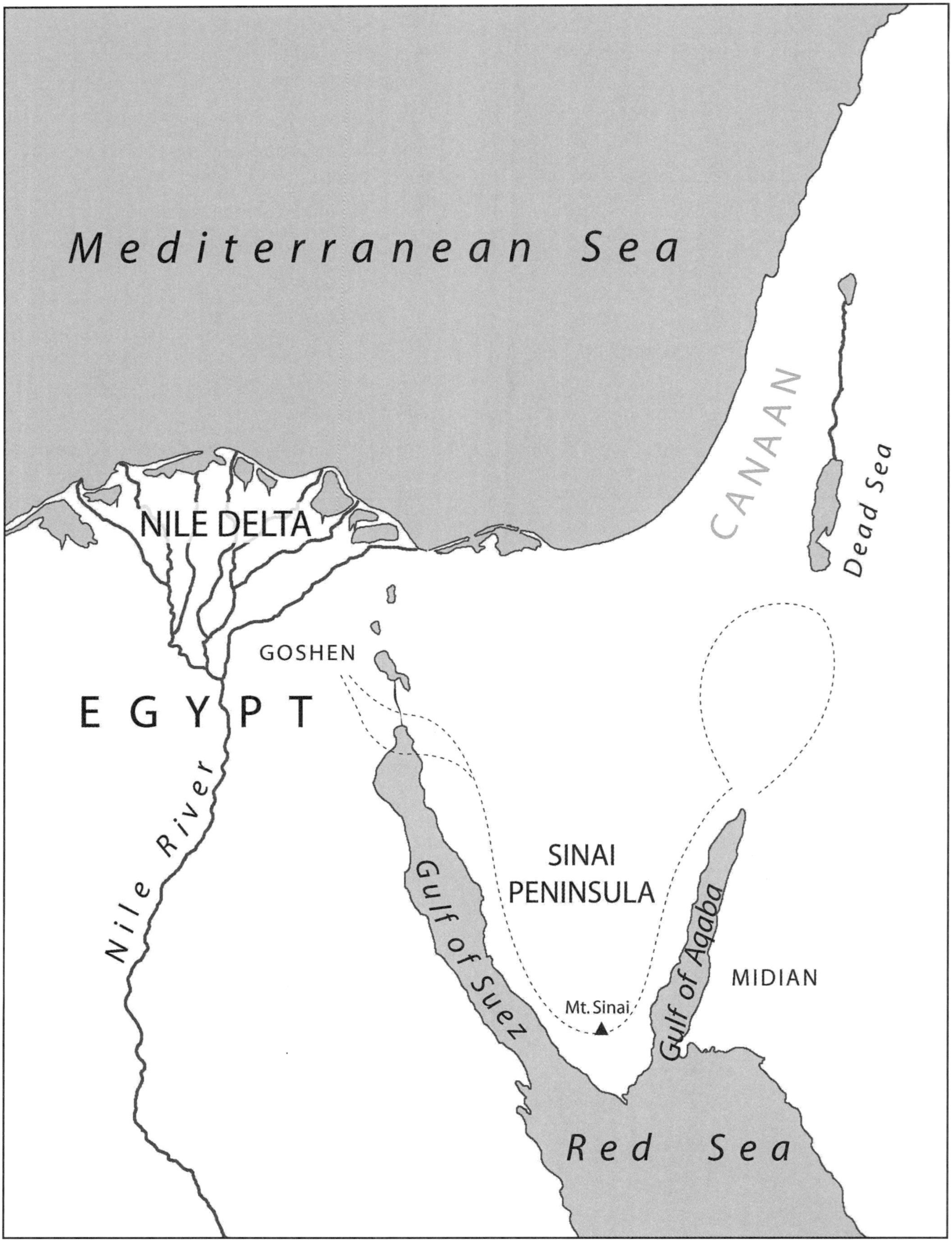
Mediterranean Sea
NILE DELTA
CANAAN
Dead Sea
GOSHEN
EGYPT
Nile River
SINAI
PENINSULA
Gulf of Suez
Gulf of Aqaba
MIDIAN
Mt. Sinai
Red Sea

Notes

LEVITICUS

Key People:

Aaron and his sons ______ are set apart for the Priesthood.

Key Terms:

High Priest: Spiritual head of Israel; only one who could enter Holy of Holies; represented the people before God

holy: separate from evil; set apart

consecrate: set apart for God's use; make holy

atonement: satisfaction for wrongdoing; reconciliation (specifically between man and God)

Outline:

1. Israel must make atonement for their sins by offering sacrifices. (Lev. 7: 37-38)
2. Aaron and his sons are consecrated for the role of priests. (Lev. 8)
3. God gives rules for cleanliness and the practice of holiness. (Lev. 17-27)

NUMBERS

Key People:

1. The faithful spies that brought back a good report of the Promised Land:
   Joshua and Caleb
2. A pagan prophet hired to curse Israel: Balaam

Key Terms:

faithful: true to accomplish what has been promised

land flowing with milk and honey: land that is fertile and characterized by abundance

Outline:

1. God punishes Israel for being unfaithful and the people are forced to wander the wilderness for ____ 40 years ____. (Numbers 14:33-35)
2. Balaam is hired to curse the Israelites, but God caused him to bless the people by causing his ____ donkey ____ to speak to him. (Numbers 22)

DEUTERONOMY

Key People:

This is the final exhortation to Israel given by ____ Moses ____.

Key Terms:

"Hear, O Israel: The Lord our God, the Lord is one" (Deut. 6:4) ____ Shema ____

Outline:

1. The book is comprised of Moses' farewell message to the people by clarifying the ____ law ____ and recounting the history of ____ Israel ____.
2. The ____ Ten Commandments ____ are repeated. (Deut. 5:1-21)
3. ____ Moses ____ is not allowed to enter the Promised Land. (Deut. 31:1-6)
4. ____ Joshua ____ succeeds Moses as the leader of Israel. (Deut. 31:7-8, 23)

Memory Verse:

Numbers 6:24-26

The Lord bless thee and keep thee: The Lord make his face shine upon thee and be gracious unto thee: The Lord lift up his countenance upon thee and give thee peace.

REVIEW: INTRODUCTION - DEUTERONOMY

Timeline: Fill in the correct date associated with the event.

2000 B.C.	The call of Abraham
1400 B.C.	The Exodus

Key People: Fill in the correct person associated with the description.

Moses	author of Pentateuch
Adam & Eve	first human beings
Noah	man whom God used to preserve mankind during the flood
Joseph	man whom God used to preserve Israel during the famine in Egypt
Pharaoh	refused to free the people of Israel
Aaron	first High Priest of Israel
Joshua and Caleb	faithful spies

Facts to Know: Fill in the correct answer associated with description.

49/39/46	number of books in the Old Testament
27	number of books in the New Testament
inspiration	doctrine that the Bible was completely guided and directed by God
Septuagint	Greek translation of the Hebrew scriptures
Tanak	the Jewish name for the Old Testament
6	number of days God took to create the world
the Fall	the event in which sin entered the world
Tower of Babel	where God confused the language of man
Canaan	land promised to Abraham and his descendents
Sodom and Gomorrah	cities destroyed by God
Isaac	offered as a sacrifice by his father
Israel	name given to Jacob
burning bush	what God appeared in to call to Moses
10 plagues	punishment sent by God against the Egyptians

Mt. Sinai	where God gives Moses the Ten Commandments
sacrifices	what Israel must offer for their sins
priests	Aaron and his sons are consecrated for what role?
40	number of years the Israelites wandered the wilderness
Balaam	God spoke to him through his donkey
Moses	was not allowed to enter the Promised Land
Joshua	succeeded Moses as leader of Israel

The Ten Commandments: Write out the Ten Commandments in the correct order.

1.	I am the Lord your God: you shall have no gods before me.	I am the Lord your God: you shall have no gods before me.
2.	You shall not take the name of the Lord your God in vain.	You shall not make any graven images.
3.	Remember the Sabbath and keep it holy.	You shall not take the name of the Lord your God in vain.
4.	Honor thy father and mother.	Remember the Sabbath and keep it holy.
5.	Thou shall not kill.	Honor thy father and mother.
6.	Thou shall not commit adultery.	You shall not kill.
7.	Thou shall not steal.	You shall not commit adultery.
8.	Thou shall not bear false witness against your neighbor.	You shall not steal.
9.	Thou shall not covet your neighbor's wife.	You shall not bear false witness against your neighbor.
10.	Thou shall not covet your neighbor's goods.	You shall not covet thy neighbor's house nor his wife nor anything that belongs to him.

↑ **Catholic/Lutheran** ↑ **Protestant**

REVIEW: INTRODUCTION - DEUTERONOMY

Vocabulary:

imago Dei	atonement	consecrate	covenant
creatio ex nihilo	faithful	holy	patriarch
redemption	tabernacle		

patriarch	head of a tribe or family
redemption	rescue, deliverance
imago Dei	image of God
creatio ex nihilo	creation out of nothing
consecrate	set apart for God's use; make holy
holy	separate from evil; set apart
covenant	a binding agreement or treaty between two parties
tabernacle	tent, center of worship for the Hebrews
atonement	satisfaction for wrongdoing
faithful	true to accomplish what has been promised

Scripture Memorization: Write the Scripture verse from memory. Be accurate.

Genesis 1:26-28 And God said, Let us make man in our image, after our likeness; and let them have dominion over the fish of the sea, and over the fowl of the air, and over the cattle, and over all the earth. So God created man in his own image, in the image of God created he him; male and female created he them. And God blessed them, and God said unto them, Be fruitful, and multiply, and replenish the earth, and subdue it.

Genesis 12:1-3 Now the Lord said unto Abram, Get thee out of thy country and from thy kindred and from thy father's house, unto a land that I will show thee; And I will make of thee a great nation and I will bless thee, and in thee shall all families of the earth be blessed.

Exodus 3:13-14 And Moses said unto God, Behold, when I come unto the children of Israel and shall say unto them, The God of your fathers has sent me unto you and they shall say unto me, What is his name? What shall I say unto them? And God said unto Moses, I AM THAT I AM; and he said, Thus shalt you say unto the children of Israel, I AM hath sent me unto you.

Numbers 6:24-26 The Lord bless thee and keep thee: The Lord make his face shine upon thee and be gracious unto thee: The Lord lift up his countenance upon thee and give thee peace.

JOSHUA

Author: Joshua

Time period covered within the book: c. 14th century B.C.

Key People:

1. The one who leads Israel in the conquest of the promised land: Joshua
2. A harlot (woman of low morals) who hides spies from Israel protecting them from harm: Rahab

Key Terms:

conquest: a success or triumph over an enemy in battle or war

obedience: conforming to the requirements set forth by God

Outline:

1. God holds back the waters as the people of Israel cross the Jordan River. (Joshua 3)
2. Israel obeys God's instruction and overcomes the great city of Jericho. (Joshua 6:1-27)
3. After conquering the Promised Land*, the land is distributed among the tribes. (Joshua 13:1-14)

*"Canaan" and/or "the land of milk and honey" are also acceptable.

JUDGES

Author: Samuel

Time period covered within the book: c. 1350-1050 B.C.

Key People:

1. Israel is delivered from the Canaanites by: Deborah
2. Israel is delivered from the Midianites by: Gideon
3. Israel is delivered from the Philistines by: Samson

Key Terms:

judge: men and women used by God to deliver Israel from oppression through military means

apostasy: a total desertion of or departure from God's commandments

Theocracy: government in Israel during the time of the Judges when God was king

Outline:

1. Israel fails to drive out all the foreign nations and suffers. (Judges 1:27-36)
2. Due to their sin, Israel would fall victim to the surrounding nations, and during this period God raised up 12 judges to deliver the people once they had repented of their wrong. (Judges 2:11-23)

Circular Nature of Judges:

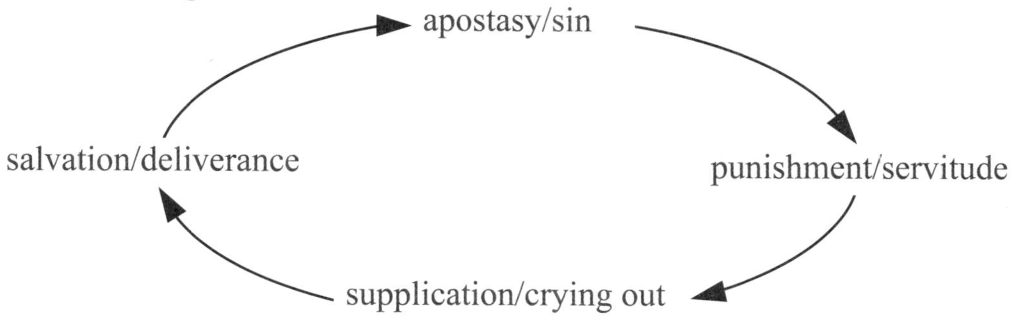

RUTH

Author: Hebrew tradition ascribes it to Samuel, though scholars are uncertain.

Time period covered within the book: c. 1350-1050

Key People:

1. left destitute by the death of her husband and sons: Naomi
2. daughter-in-law of Naomi who chooses stay with her: Ruth
3. the kinsman-redeemer who marries Ruth: Boaz
4. the child of Boaz and Ruth and future grandfather of David: Obed

Key Terms:

kinsman-redeemer: a relative who preserves the family name and land of a widowed woman

Memory Verse:

Ruth 1:16

And Ruth said, Entreat me not to leave thee, or to return from following after thee; for whither thou goest, I will go, and where thou lodgest I will lodge: thy people shall be my people, and thy God, my God.

I & II SAMUEL

Author: Hebrew tradition ascribes it to Samuel though scholars are uncertain.

Time period covered within the book: 1050 - 971 B.C.

Key People:

1. Prophet of God and final judge of Israel: Samuel
2. The first king of Israel: Saul
3. Slayer of Goliath and second king of Israel: David
4. Son of Saul who protects David from his father: Jonathan
5. The wife David took from Uriah: Bathsheba
6. God's prophet to David: Nathan
7. Son of David who tries to take the throne: Absalom

Key Terms:

monarchy: a state or nation ruled by a monarch or a king

Outline:

1. The Ark of the Covenant is stolen by the Philistines, but God brings such plague against them that they return it after seven months. (I Samuel 5-6:9)
2. The people demand that God give them a king, and God has Samuel anoint Saul. (I Samuel 8:1-9; 9:15-21; 10:1-8)
3. Israel goes to battle with the Philistines, and their champion, Goliath, is defeated by David. (I Samuel 17)
4. Saul loses his three sons in battle with the Philistines and commits suicide. (I Samuel 31:1-7)
5. David becomes king of Israel and builds his capital city in Jerusalem. (II Samuel 5:1-5)
6. God makes a covenant with David that his throne will be an eternal throne. (II Samuel 7:1-17)
7. Though David should be with his troops in battle, he tarries and steals Bathsheba, the wife of Uriah the Hittite. (II Samuel 11:1-26)

8. David's own son, Absalom, revolts against him and is slain in battle.

(II Samuel 18:1-15)

Memory Verse:

I Samuel 17:45-46

Then David said to the Philistine, Thou comest to me with a sword, and with a spear, and with a shield: but I come to thee in the name of the Lord of hosts. ... This day will the Lord deliver thee into mine hand; and I will smite thee ... that all the earth may know that there is a God in Israel.

Map of Canaan during Saul's and David's rule:

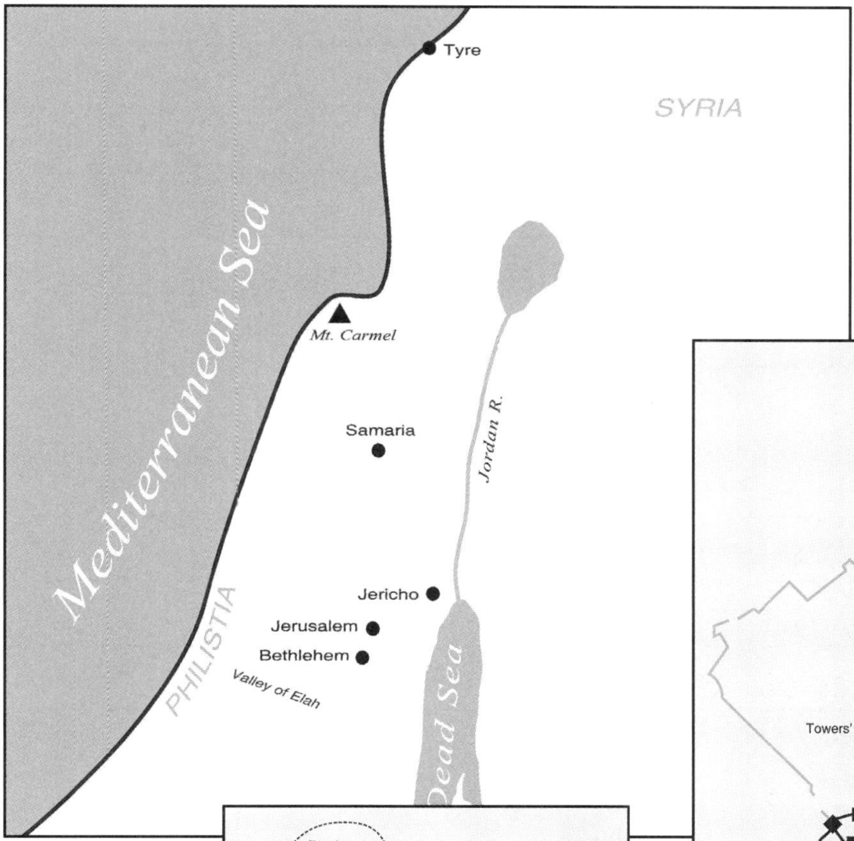

Jerusalem at the time of Jesus:

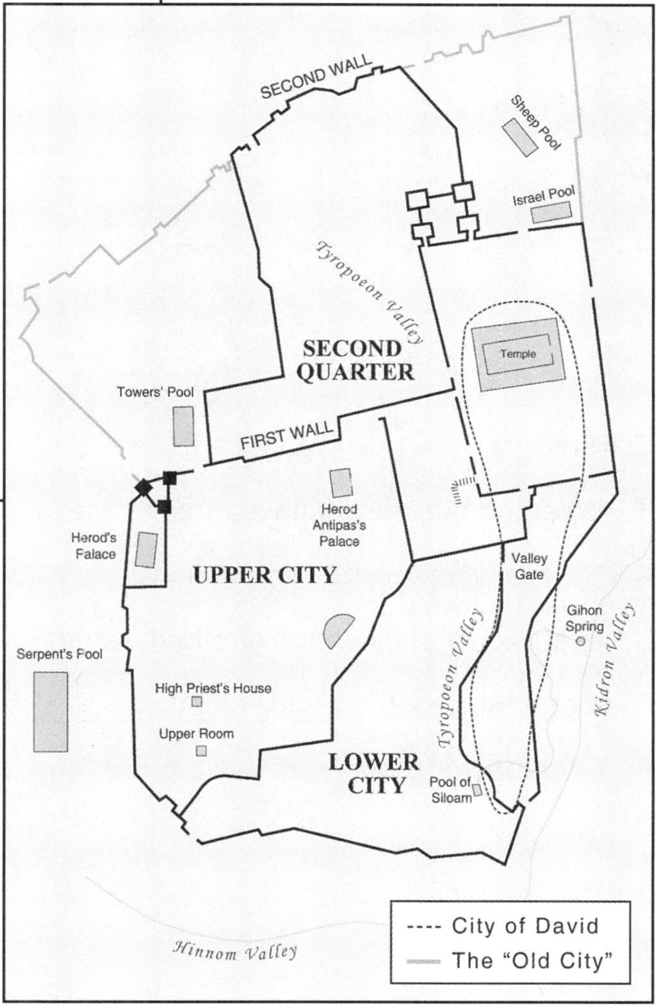

City of David:

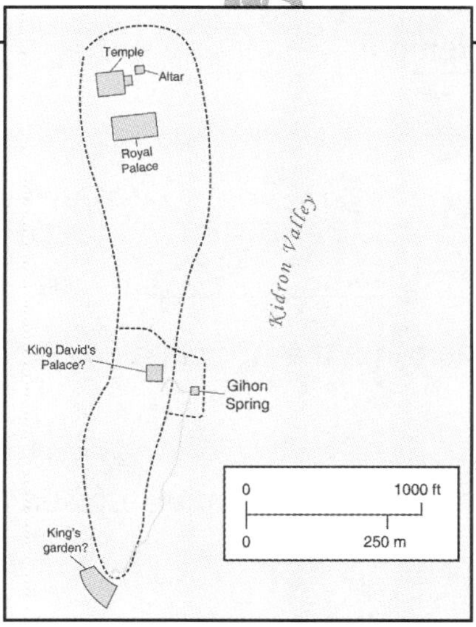

I & II KINGS

Author: Hebrew tradition ascribes it to ___Jeremiah___ though scholars are uncertain

Time period covered within the book: ___970-586 B.C.___

Key People:

1. David's son that inherited the throne; built the temple and a palace: ___Solomon___
2. First king of the Northern Kingdom: ___Jeroboam I___
3. First king of the Southern Kingdom: ___Rehoboam___
4. The most evil of the kings of Israel (1 Kings 16:33): ___Ahab___
5. Ahab's evil wife who killed the prophets of God: ___Jezebel___
6. The prophet sent to punish Ahab: ___Elijah___
7. The prophet who took the place of Elijah: ___Elisha___
8. The king of Judah who repaired the temple and reformed Judah according to the Book of the Law: ___Josiah___

Key Terms:

temple: ___permanent structure, center of Hebrew worship___

sovereignty: ___Supremacy of authority or rule; God is in control of history___

division: ___Israel is separated into two kingdoms___

exile: ___forced removal from one's native land___

Outline:

1. Solomon becomes king and builds the ___temple___, which is the center of Israel's worship. (I Kings 6:1-14, 37-38)
2. Israel is divided into the Northern Kingdom, called ___Israel___, and the Southern Kingdom, called ___Judah___, in ___931 B.C.___. (I Kings 12:16-24)
3. Ahab becomes king of the Northern Kingdom and turns the people away from the Lord to worship ___Baal___. (I Kings 16:29-34)
4. ___Elijah___ confronts Ahab and defeats the prophets of Baal in a challenge. (I Kings 18:20-40)

5. Elijah was taken to heaven in a ___chariot of fire___, and ___Elisha___ took his place as prophet to Israel. (II Kings 2:1-18)
6. The Northern Kingdom falls to Assyria in ___722 B.C.___. (II Kings 15:29-31)
7. Josiah becomes king of Judah at the age of ___8___ and finds the ___Book of the Law___ ______. He calls the people to again be faithful to the Lord. (II Kings 22:1-7, 11-13)
8. The Southern Kingdoms falls and is exiled to Babylon in ___586 B.C.___. (II Kings 25:1-21)

Memory Verse:

I Kings 19:11-12

But the Lord was not in the wind: and after the wind an earthquake; but the Lord was not in the earthquake. And after the earthquake a fire; but the Lord was not in the fire: and after the fire a still, small voice.

The Division of Israel:

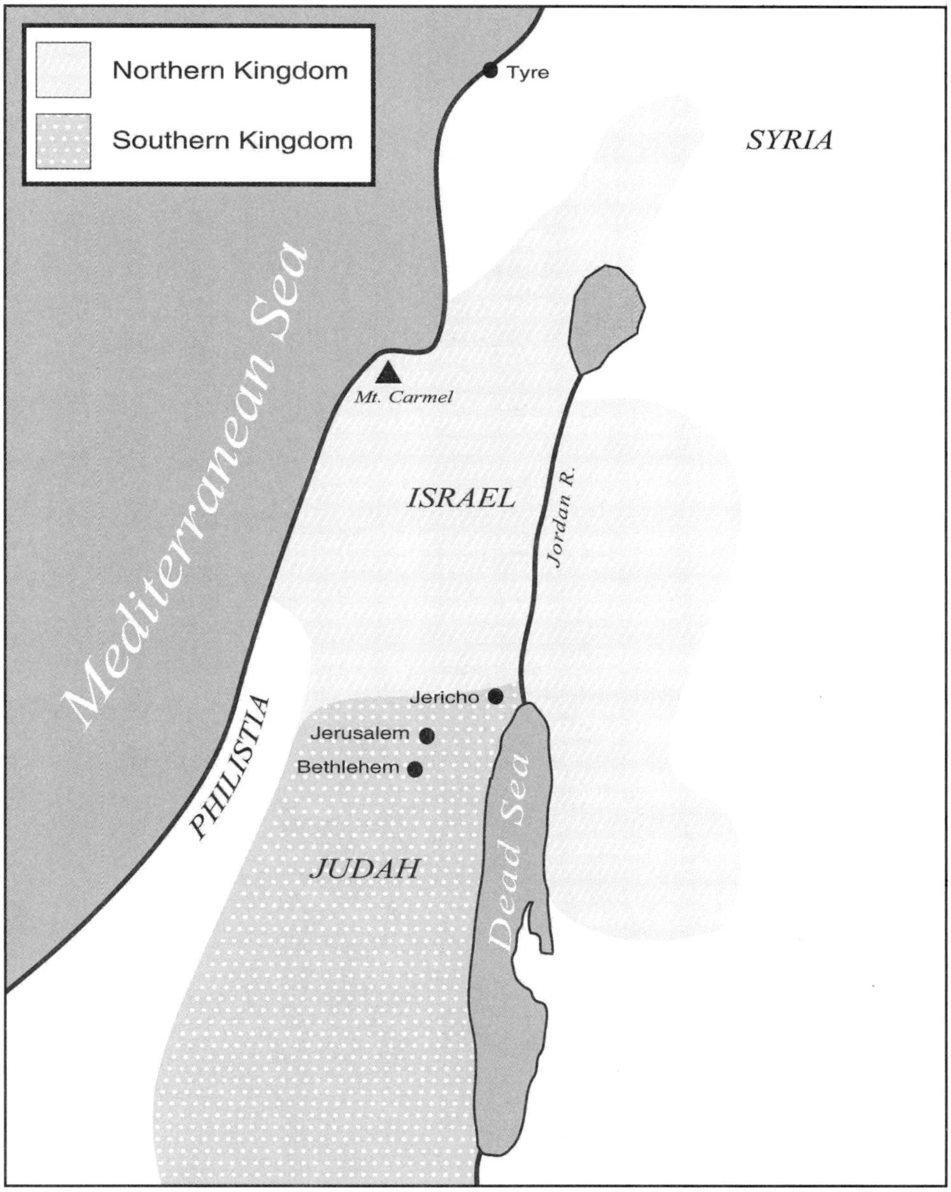

*Look for a map illustrating the Assyrian and Babylonian exiles on the following page.

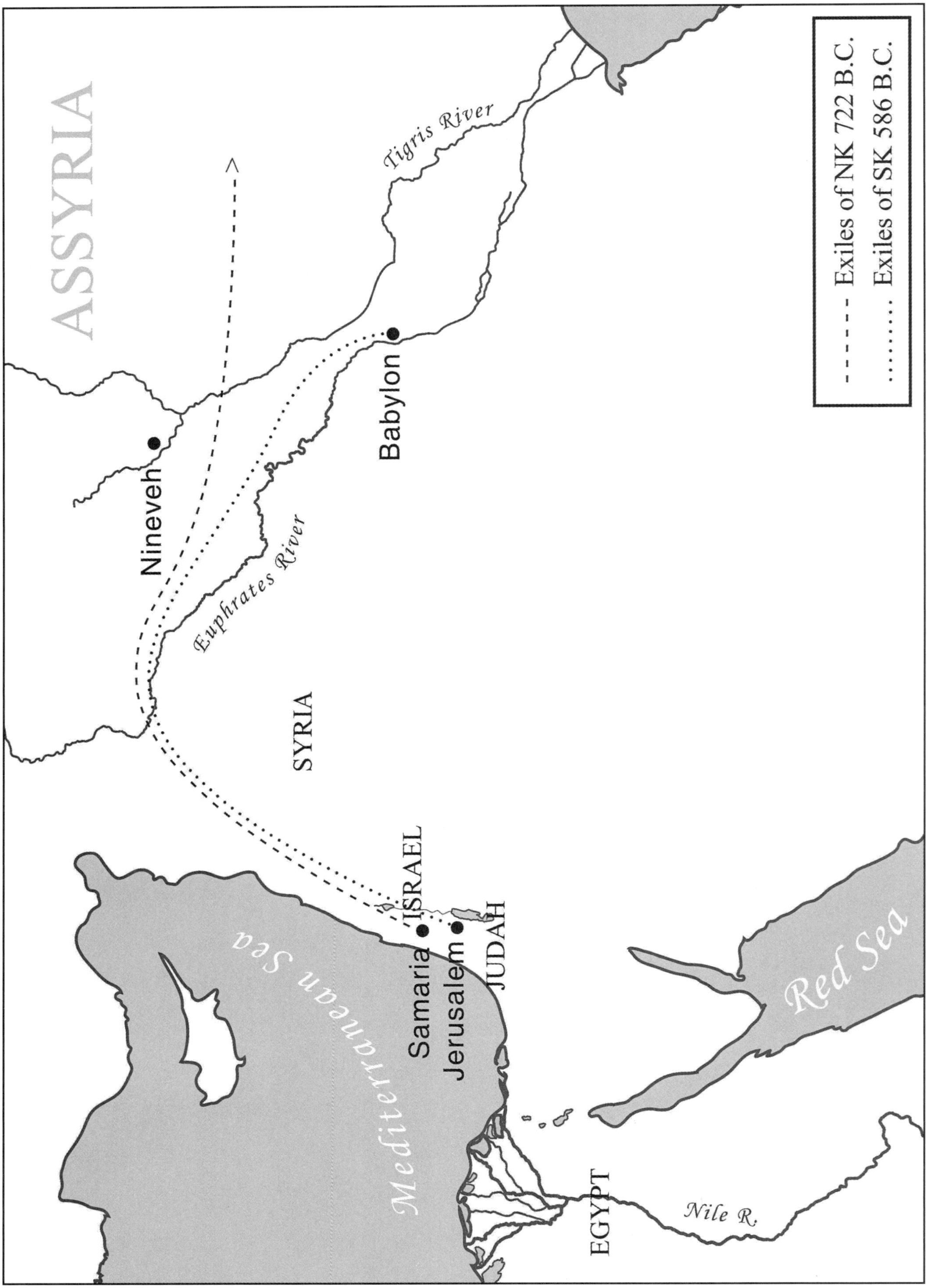
ASSYRIA
Tigris River
Nineveh
Babylon
Euphrates River
SYRIA
ISRAEL
Samaria
Jerusalem
JUDAH
Mediterranean Sea
Red Sea
EGYPT
Nile R.
Exiles of NK 722 B.C.
Exiles of SK 586 B.C.

Notes

I & II CHRONICLES

Author: Hebrew tradition ascribes it to Ezra though scholars are uncertain

Time period covered within the book: 1010 - 536 B.C.

Key Terms:

captivity: the state or period of being held, imprisoned, or enslaved

Outline:

Covers the same period as I & II Samuel and I & II Kings, starting with David and focusing on the successes of the good kings of the Southern Kingdom of Judah and condemning the sins of the bad kings in order to inspire hope for the Jews returning to Jerusalem and emphasizing the need for true worship in the temple.

EZRA - NEHEMIAH

The earliest traditions treat these books as one volume depicting the Jews' return to Jerusalem.

Author: Hebrew tradition ascribes it to Ezra though scholars are uncertain.

Time period covered within the book: 538 - 433 B.C.

Key People:

1. The Persian king who captures Babylon and lets the Jewish exiles return to Jerusalem: Cyrus
2. Led the first group of exiles who returned: Sheshbazzar
3. Community leaders who began rebuilding the altar and the temple: Zerubbabel and Jeshua
4. The scribe and priest who led the second group of returning exiles and restored the Law: Ezra
5. Royal cupbearer and leader of the third and final group of returning exiles: Nehemiah
6. The Persian king who released Ezra and Nehemiah to rebuild the walls of Jerusalem: Artaxerxes

Key Terms:

restoration: the act of restoring; renewal, revival, or reestablishment

Outline:

1. Babylon is conquered by Persia in 539 B.C., and the exiles first return to Jerusalem in 536 B.C. after Cyrus' decree. (Ezra 1)
2. Upon their return, Zerubbabel and Jeshua lead the people in rebuilding the altar and the temple. (Ezra 3)
3. Ezra establishes spiritual restoration by establishing the Law of Moses and true worship among the people. (Ezra 7:1-20)
4. Nehemiah establishes political restoration by overseeing the rebuilding of the walls of Jerusalem. (Nehemiah 2:1-16)

ESTHER

Author: Scholars are uncertain.

Time period covered within the book: sometime during the reign of Xerxes 484-464 B.C.

Key People:

1. In this book the King of Persia, Xerxes, is referred to by his Persian name: Ahasuerus
2. Hebrew girl who was chosen to be queen of Persia: Esther
3. An official of King Ahasuerus who devised a plot to kill all the Jews: Haman
4. The Jew who overheard the plot to kill the king and, with Esther, saved the Jews: Mordecai

Key Terms:

providence: the foreseeing care and guidance of God in the affairs of man

Outline:

Though the book of Esther doesn't mention the name of God, His provision is evident in the circumstances surrounding the preservation of the Jews.

Memory Verse:

Ezra 7:27

Blessed be the Lord God of our fathers, which hath put such a thing as this in the king's heart, to beautify the house of the Lord which is in Jerusalem.

REVIEW: JOSHUA - ESTHER

Timeline: Fill in the correct date associated with the event.

931 BC	Israel is divided into the Northern and Southern Kingdoms
722 BC	Northern Kingdom falls to Assyria
586 BC	Southern Kingdom falls to Babylon
536 BC	Exiles first return to Jerusalem

Key People: Fill in the correct person associated with the description.

Rahab	prostitute who hid Israelite spies
Deborah	delivered Israel from the Canaanites
Gideon	delivered Israel from the Midianites
Samson	delivered Israel from the Philistines
Ruth	daughter-in-law of Naomi who chooses to stay with her
Boaz	kinsman-redeemer who marries Ruth
Samuel	prophet of God and final judge of Israel
Saul	first king of Israel
David	slayer of Goliath; second king of Israel
Jonathan	son of Saul who protects David from his father
Bathsheba	wife David took from Uriah
Nathan	God's prophet to David
Absalom	son of David who tries to take his throne
Solomon	son of David; built temple and palace
Jereboam I	first king of Northern Kingdom
Rehoboam	first king of Southern Kingdom
Elijah	prophet taken in a chariot of fire
Elisha	prophet who took the place of Elijah
Cyrus	Persian king who captures Babylon and lets exiles return
Ezra	scribe and priest who led the second group of exiles and restored the Law

Nehemiah — royal cupbearer; led third group of exiles

Artaxerxes — Persian king who released Ezra and Nehemiah to rebuild walls

Esther — Hebrew girl who was chosen as queen of Persia

Haman — devised a plot to kill all the Jews

Mordecai — Jew who helped Esther save the Jews

Facts to Know: Fill in the correct answer associated with description.

Jericho — city that Israel defeated after crossing the Jordan River

Jerusalem — place where David builds his capital city

Israel — name of the Northern Kingdom

Judah — name of the Southern Kingdom

The Circular Nature of Judges: Complete the diagram.

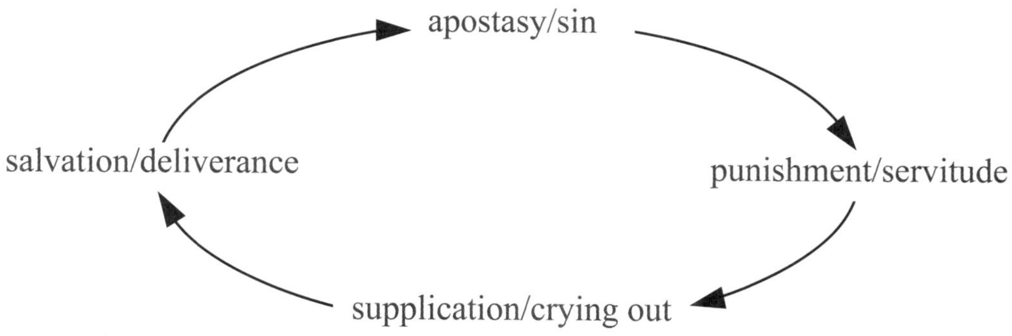

REVIEW: JOSHUA - ESTHER

Vocabulary:

apostasy	captivity	conquest	division
exile	judge	kinsman-redeemer	monarchy
obedience	providence	restoration	sovereignty
temple	Theocracy		

conquest	success over an enemy in battle
obedience	conforming to the requirements set forth by God
judge	deliverer of Israel primarily through military means
apostasy	total departure from God's commandments
Theocracy	government in Israel during the time of the Judges when God was king
kinsman redeemer	a relative who preserves the family and land of a widowed woman
monarchy	state or nation ruled by a monarch or king
temple	permanent structure, center of Hebrew worship
sovereignty	supremacy of authority or rule
division	Israel is separated into two kingdoms
exile	forced removal from one's native land
captivity	state of being imprisoned or enslaved
restoration	renewal, revival, or reestablishment
providence	the foreseeing care and guidance of God in the affairs of man

Scripture Memorization: Write the Scripture verse from memory. Be accurate.

Ruth 1:16 And Ruth said, Entreat me not to leave thee, or to return from following after thee; for whither thou goest, I will go, and where thou lodgest I will lodge: thy people shall be my people, and thy God, my God.

I Samuel 17:45-46 Then David said to the Philistine, Thou comest to me with a sword, and with a spear, and with a shield: but I come to thee in the name of the Lord of hosts. … This day will the Lord deliver thee into mine hand; and I will smite thee … that all the earth may know that there is a God in Israel.

I Kings 19:11-12 But the Lord was not in the wind: and after the wind an earthquake; but the Lord was not in the earthquake. And after the earthquake a fire; but the Lord was not in the fire: and after the fire a still, small voice.

Ezra 7:27 Blessed be the Lord God of our fathers, which hath put such a thing as this in the king's heart, to beautify the house of the Lord which is in Jerusalem.

THE PROPHETS

For the purpose of this course each prophet will be handled in relation to the time period in which he served. Each book within the prophetic writings is titled after the prophet who wrote it.

1. The prophets: men called by God to speak for God and guide His people
2. The focus of the prophets' message was always to call the people to repent/turn back to their loving God who would accept them and forgive their sin.
3. In the Old Testament the writings of the prophets are organized into two sections; the Major Prophets and the Minor Prophets. The terms "major" and "minor" simply refer to the length of the prophet's book and not to its importance.

PRE-FALL OF THE NORTHERN KINGDOM OF ISRAEL

The following prophets ministered in the Northern Kingdom in the time leading up to its fall to Assyria.

AMOS

Time period covered within the book: c. 760-739 B.C.

Key Terms:

justice: conformity to moral rightness in action or attitude; righteousness

Outline:

1. God demands that Israel and even the surrounding nations should treat others justly.
2. God promises judgment for Israel's failure to demonstrate justice. (Amos 2:1-8)
3. The fall of the Northern and Southern Kingdoms is foretold. (Amos 9:1-10)

JONAH

Time period during which the prophet ministered: c. 760-750 B.C.

Key Terms:

compassion: sympathy for the misfortune of others and a desire to help them

Nineveh: capital city of Assyria

Outline:

1. Jonah is commissioned to go to Nineveh and tell them to turn from their sin, but he flees instead. (Jonah 1:1-3)
2. Jonah was punished by being thrown overboard and swallowed by a fish, in which he stayed for three days and nights. (Jonah 1:4-17)
3. God shows love and mercy for Nineveh and spares the city when the people repent. (Jonah 3:6-10)

Memory Verses:

Amos 5:24

But let judgment run down as waters, and righteousness as a mighty stream.

Jonah 3:10

And God saw their works, that they turned from their evil way; and God repented of the evil, that he had said that he would do unto them; and he did it not.

Map of Nineveh and Tarshish: *Look on the following page.

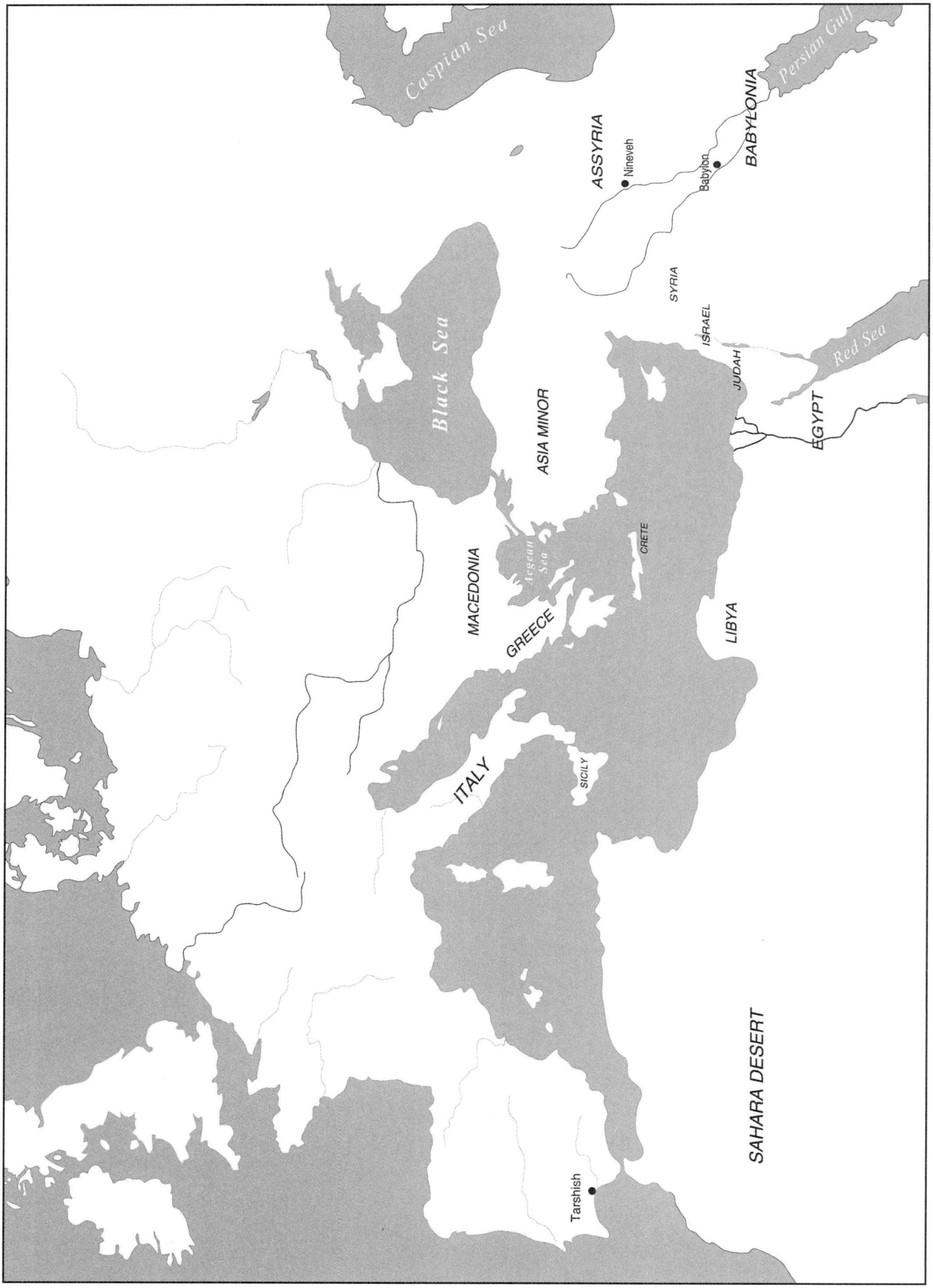
Caspian Sea
Persian Gulf
ASSYRIA
Nineveh
Babylon
BABYLONIA
Black Sea
SYRIA
ISRAEL
JUDAH
Red Sea
ASIA MINOR
EGYPT
Aegean Sea
CRETE
MACEDONIA
GREECE
LIBYA
ITALY
SICILY
SAHARA DESERT
Tarshish

Notes

FALL OF THE NORTHERN KINGDOM OF ISRAEL

Hosea ministered in the Northern kingdom during its fall.
Micah and Isaiah ministered in the Southern Kingdom during the fall of the Northern Kingdom.

HOSEA

Time period during which the prophet ministered: c. 755-720 B.C.

Key People:

1. The prophet whose life reflected God's relationship with Israel: Hosea
2. The unfaithful wife of Hosea: Gomer

Key Terms:

unfaithful: failing to act in accordance with the Law

Outline:

1. God uses Hosea's marriage as a metaphor for His relationship with Israel. (Hosea 1:2-3)
2. Just as Hosea's wife, Gomer, was unfaithful to Hosea, so also Israel has been unfaithful to God by worshipping Baal.
3. God promises to punish both the Northern and Southern Kingdoms for their unfaithfulness. (Hosea 5)
4. Hosea pleads with the people of Israel to return to the Lord and find healing. ______. (Hosea 14)

MICAH

Time period during which the prophet ministered: c. 740-700 B.C.

Key Terms:

indictment: an accusation of guilt by listing out the crimes of the guilty party

remnant: a small surviving group of people

Outline:

1. Micah lays all the sins of the Northern and Southern Kingdoms before them and tells them of God's coming judgment. (Micah 1:2-7)
2. God, in His mercy, promises to save a remnant of the people of Israel and provide them with a new ruler/Messianic King. (Micah 5)

ISAIAH

Time period during which the prophet ministered: c. 740-681 B.C.

Key Terms:

Messiah: the promised deliverer of Israel

Outline:

1. Isaiah foretells the judgment of God on the Northern and Southern Kingdoms, including Babylon's capture of Jerusalem. (Isaiah 3:1-5, 8-12)
2. Israel foretells the judgment of God on the surrounding nations and the world. (Isaiah 13:9-11)
3. Isaiah foretells God's preservation of the remnant of Israel and the destruction of Babylon. (Isaiah 48:1-11, 20-22)
4. Isaiah reveals God's plan to ultimately to display His glory by restoring Israel and blessing the world through the Messiah. (Isaiah 9:1-7; 52:13- 53:12)

Memory Verse:

Isaiah 9:2,6

The people that walked in darkness have seen a great light. For unto us a child is born, unto us a son is given: and the government shall be upon his shoulder; and his name shall be called Wonderful, Counsellor, The mighty God, The everlasting Father, The Prince of Peace.

THE FALL OF THE SOUTHERN KINGDOM OF JUDAH

Nahum, Habakkuk, and Zephania all ministered in the time between the fall of the Northern Kingdom and the fall of the Southern Kingdom. Jeremiah ministered before and during the event of the fall of the Southern Kingdom.

NAHUM

Time period this book covers: c. 640-609 B.C.

Outline:

Nahum is called by God to go to Nineveh to proclaim to them their impending destruction because of turning from the Lord. (Nahum 1:1-14)

HABAKKUK

Time period during which the prophet ministered: c. 640-609 B.C.

Key Terms:

dialogue: conversation between one or more persons.

Outline:

1. Habakkuk, in his dialogue with God, complains about the injustice he sees around him, and God replies by revealing his plan to punish Judah through Babylon. (Habakkuk 1:2-6)
2. Habakkuk wonders how God can use an evil nation to judge His people, and God explains that He judges all sin at the right time. (Habakkuk 1:12-13; 2:3)

ZEPHANIAH

Time period during which the prophet ministered: c. 640-609 B.C.

Key Terms:

Day of the Lord: the final day of judgment

Outline:

1. Zephaniah declares the coming final judgment of all nations called the Day of the Lord. (Zephaniah 1:7-9, 17-18)

2. Those who turn back to God will be blessed and not be destroyed.

(Zephaniah 3:14-20)

JEREMIAH

Time period during which the prophet ministered: c. 627-586 B.C.

Key Terms:

repent: feeling remorse for one's sins and changing one's behavior

Outline:

1. Jeremiah pleads with Judah to repent from their sins but foresees Jerusalem's destruction at the hand of Babylon. (Jeremiah 3:11-14; 10:17-25)
2. Jeremiah assures the people of God that He will restore them after the judgment and fulfill His promise to David. (Jeremiah 30:10-11; 33:14-18)
3. Jeremiah witnesses the fall of Jerusalem and the destruction of the temple. (Jeremiah 52:4-15)

LAMENTATIONS

Author: Jeremiah

Key Terms:

lament: an expression of grief or sorrow

Outline:

Lamentations was written as a song to seek God's forgiveness, mourn the destruction of the temple, and ask that He restore His people. (Lamentations 5:1-8,19-21)

Memory Verse:

Jeremiah 31:31-33

Behold, the days come, saith the Lord, that I will make a new covenant with the house of Israel and the house of Judah: Not according to the covenant I made with their fathers; which my covenant they break, but I will put a new law in their inward parts, and write it in their hearts; and I will be their God, and they shall be my people.

JUDAH IN EXILE

These prophets ministered to the Jews exiled to Babylon.

OBADIAH

Time period during which the prophet ministered: c. 586-553 B.C.

Outline:

1. Edom had raided Jerusalem while it was being sacked by the Babylonians, and Obadiah prophesied the judgment and destruction of Edom. (Obadiah 10-11, 15)
2. Obadiah prophesied the restoration of Judah in the Promised Land. (Obadiah 20-21)

DANIEL

Time period this book covers: c. 605-536 B.C.

Key Terms:

vision: a vivid picture of reality given to man by God that can't be seen without His help

Outline:

1. Daniel's three friends, Shadrach, Meshach, and Abednego, are thrown into a fiery furnace for refusing to worship the statue of Nebuchadnezzar that he built himself, but God preserves them. (Daniel 3:8-30)
2. Daniel warns King Belshazzar of the coming invasion by the Medes and Persians by reading the writing on the wall. (Daniel 5:24-31)
3. Daniel was thrown into the lion's den for praying to God instead of King Darius, and Daniel trusted God and wasn't harmed. (Daniel 6:14-24)
4. Daniel was given a vision of the final judgment of all the earth. (Daniel 12:1-3)

EZEKIEL

Time period during which the prophet ministered: c. 593-571 B.C.

Key Terms:

culpable: deserving blame for wrongdoing

Outline:

1. Ezekiel looks at the judgment of Israel and Judah and proclaims the future judgment of the surrounding nations. (Ezekiel 25-32)
2. Ezekiel explains that Judah is culpable for the judgment they are receiving. (Ezekiel 39:21-24)
3. Ezekiel is given a vision of God's restoration of His people. (Ezekiel 39:25-29)

JOEL

Time period this book covers: Scholars are uncertain- probably sometime after 586 B.C..

Outline:

1. Joel describes the coming Day of the Lord during which Judah and all other nations will be judged. (Joel 2:1-2,11; 3:1-2)
2. However, the Day of the Lord will be a time of restoration for those who repent and return to the Lord. (Joel 2:12-14, 32)

Memory Verse:

Joel 2:32

And it shall come to pass, that whosoever shall call on the name of the LORD shall be delivered.

EXILES RETURN TO JERUSALEM

Haggai and Zechariah ministered to the first group of exiles to return to Jerusalem during the rebuilding of the temple. Malachi ministered after the return of the second group of exiles following the completion of the temple.

HAGGAI

Time period during which the prophet ministered: 520 B.C.

Key Terms:

perseverance: continuing in a course of action in spite of difficulties or discouragement

Outline:

Though opposition had risen against the building of the temple, Haggai encourages the people to persevere and complete the work because it will please God and they will receive His presence. (Haggai 1:7-11; 2:4-9)

ZECHARIAH

Time period during which the prophet ministered: 520-518 B.C.

Key Terms:

shepherd: a person who predicts, protects, guides, or watches over a person or a group of people

Outline:

1. Zechariah challenges the people to remain faithful to the Lord and complete the building of the temple. (Zechariah 1:3-6)
2. Zechariah prophesies that a king will again reign in Jerusalem and bring judgment against the nations that oppressed Israel. (Zechariah 9:9)
3. God's shepherd will restore His people and cleanse them of their idolatry. (Zechariah 13:7-9)

MALACHI

Time period during which the prophet ministered: c. 460 B.C.

Key Terms:

fidelity: faithfulness to obligations and commitments

Outline:

1. Malachi challenges the people to remember the Law of Moses and renew their commitment to be faithful to its requirements. (Malachi 3:16-18; 4:4)
2. Malachi encourages the people to remember that the Day of the Lord is coming and that he will preserve those who fear His name. (Malachi 4:1-3)

Memory Verse:

Zechariah 7:9-10

Thus speaketh the LORD of hosts, saying, Execute true judgment, and show mercy and compassions every man to his brother: And oppress not the widow, nor the fatherless, the stranger, nor the poor; and let none of you imagine evil against his brother in your heart.

REVIEW: THE PROPHETS

Facts to Know: Fill in the correct answer associated with description.

prophets	men called by God to speak for God and guide His people
Major Prophets	section of Bible containing prophets with longer books
Minor Prophets	section of Bible containing prophets with shorter books
Gomer	unfaithful wife of Hosea
Nebuchadnezzar	king who built a golden statue of himself
Darius	king who threw Daniel in the lion's den
repent	the primary message of the prophets
3	number of days Jonah was in the belly of the fish

Old Testament Prophets: Fill in the prophets that fit the descriptions.

Amos	first to foretell the fall of the Northern and Southern Kingdoms
Jonah	first prophet sent to Nineveh; swallowed by a fish
Hosea	prophet whose life reflected God's relationship with Israel
Micah	prophet's book was an indictment of Israel
Isaiah	revealed God's plan to restore Israel and bless the world through the Messiah
Nahum	second prophet sent to Nineveh
Habakkuk	prophet whose book is a dialogue between himself and God
Zephaniah	first prophet to describe the coming final judgment of all nations
Jeremiah	prophet who witnessed the fall of Jerusalem
Lamentations	book written by Jeremiah mourning the destruction of the temple
Obadiah	foretold the destruction of Edom for raiding Jerusalem
Daniel	given a vision of the final judgment
Ezekiel	demonstrated that Judah deserved the judgment they received
Joel	prophet who described the coming Day of the Lord and called Judah to repent
Haggai	encouraged the people to persevere in rebuilding the temple

Zechariah — spoke of a coming Shepherd who would guide God's people

Malachi — challenged the people to remember the Law of Moses

Vocabulary:

compassion	culpable	Day of the Lord	dialogue
fidelity	indictment	justice	lament
Messiah	perseverance	remnant	repent
shepherd	unfaithful	vision	

justice — conformity to moral rightness

compassion — sympathy for the misfortune of others; desire to help

unfaithful — failing to act in accordance with the Law

indictment — an accusation of guilt

remnant — a small surviving group of people

Messiah — the promised deliverer of Israel

dialogue — conversation between one or more persons

Day of the Lord — the final day of judgment

repent — feeling remorse and changing one's behavior

lament — an expression of grief or sorrow

vision — a vivid picture of reality that can't be seen without God's help

culpable — deserving blame for wrongdoing

perserverance — continuing in a course of action in spite of difficulties

shepherd — a person who protects and guides a person or group

fidelity — faithfulness to obligations and commitments

REVIEW: THE PROPHETS

Scripture Memorization: Write the Scripture verse from memory. Be accurate.

Amos 5:24 But let judgment run down as waters, and righteousness as a mighty stream.

Jonah 3:10 And God saw their works, that they turned from their evil way; and God repented of the evil, that he had said that he would do unto them; and he did it not.

Isaiah 9:2,6 The people that walked in darkness have seen a great light. For unto us a child is born, unto us a son is given: and the government shall be upon his shoulder; and his name shall be called Wonderful, Counsellor, The mighty God, The everlasting Father, The Prince of Peace.

Jeremiah 31:31-33 Behold, the days come, saith the Lord, that I will make a new covenant with the house of Israel and with the house of Judah: Not according to the covenant that I made with their fathers … which my covenant they break … but I will put my law in their inward parts, and write it in their hearts; and I will be their God, and they shall be my people.

Joel 2:32 And it shall come to pass, that whosoever shall call on the name of the LORD shall be delivered.

Zechariah 7:9-10 Thus speaketh the LORD of hosts, saying, Execute true judgment, and shew mercy and compassions every man to his brother: And oppress not the widow, nor the fatherless, the stranger, nor the poor; and let none of you imagine evil against his brother in your heart.

Notes

POETRY AND WISDOM LITERATURE

1. Although all of Hebrew literature is filled with poetry the Bible contains a particular section designated for poetic and wisdom writings. The books within this section are **Job**, **Psalms**, **Proverbs**, **Ecclesiastes**, and **Song of Solomon**.

2. The two general aspects of poetry are ___rhythm and rhyme___. It is important to understand that besides rhyming sounds (kick-sick, more-store) the Hebrews rhymed ideas.

   "Pride goes before destruction, and a haughty spirit before a fall" (Proverbs 16:18)

   The ideas of pride destroying and pride causing one to fall "rhyme" with each other. This special aspect of Hebrew poetry is called ___parallelism___. Hebrew parallelism consists of lines with two parts that closely relate to each other. The majority of this parallelism comes in three forms:

   A. ___Synonymous/Repeating___: The first part makes a statement and the second part repeats the statement in a different way.

   "The heavens declare the glory of God, and the sky above proclaims his handiwork." (Psalm 19:1)

   B. ___Antithetic/Opposite___: The first part makes a statement and the second part tells the opposite of that statement.

   "A soft answer turns away wrath, but a harsh word stirs up anger." (Proverbs 15:1)

   C. ___Synthetic/Completing___: The first part makes a statement and the second part completes the idea started by the first.

   "He is like a tree planted by streams of water that yields fruit in season and its leaf does not wither. In all that he does, he prospers" (Psalm 1:3)

PSALMS

Author(s): ___David___ is the author of the majority of the Psalms. Other authors are Asaph, Solomon, Moses, and the sons of Korah.

Time period covered within the book: The book of Psalms is a collection of ___poems___, ___songs___, and ___prayers___ written throughout the history of Israel. It was compiled into its final form by an editor after the return of the exiles.

Key Terms:

psalm/hymn: song of praise to God

corporate worship: all the people of God gathering together to worship God

genre: a category of artistic work; i.e., music, literature, painting

Outline:

1. The Israelites used the book of Psalms as a hymnal/song book for their corporate worship.
2. The book of Psalms is divided into 5 books that together loosely move through the history of Israel from Moses to the return from Babylon.
3. Within the book of Psalms you will encounter 150 individual songs that run the full spectrum of human emotion, particularly in dealing with man's relationship to God. The many types of songs can be classified into six basic genres.
   A. Praise: praise God for who He is and what he has done. (Psalm 145:1-9)
   B. Thanksgiving: thank God for answering prayers. (Psalm 107:1-8)
   C. Lament: express sadness/fear due to present circumstances. (Psalm 51:1-6)
   D. Confidence: express confidence and trust in God. (Psalm 23; 121)
   E. Kingship: particularly focused on God's blessing the nations through the Davidic Monarchy. (Psalm 2)
   F. Wisdom: reflect the themes found in the wisdom books (Proverbs, Job, Song of Solomon, and Ecclesiastes) (Psalm 37:1-9)

Memory Verses:

Psalm 1

Blessed is the man that walketh not in the counsel of the ungodly, nor standeth in the way of sinners, nor sitteth in the seat of the scornful. **synonymous**

But his delight is in the law of the Lord; and in his law doth he meditate day and night. **synthetic**

And he shall be like a tree planted by the rivers of water, that bringeth forth his fruit in his season; his leaf also shall not wither; and whatsoever he doeth shall prosper. **synthetic**

The ungodly are not so; but are like the chaff which the wind driveth away. **synthetic**

Therefore the ungodly shall not stand in the judgment, nor sinners in the congregation of the righteous. **synonymous**

For the Lord knoweth the way of the righteous: but the way of the ungodly shall perish. **antithetic**

BOOKS OF WISDOM

Hebrew wisdom is a type of Hebrew poetry that focuses on the correct way to live based on the way God has ordered the world. It is not a strict set of rules like the Law, but examples that aid godly living.

PROVERBS

Author(s): The majority of the book was written by ____Solomon____ with a few passages written by Agur, Lemuel, and a group called "the wise."

Key Terms:

wisdom: ____the skill of living life in a godly way____

Outline:

1. Proverbs is based on the fact that all knowledge begins with the ____fear of God____. (Proverbs 1:1-7)
2. The book of Proverbs encourages man to pursue ____wisdom____ in order to live rightly. (Proverbs 2:1-15)

ECCLESIASTES

Author: ____Solomon____

Key Terms:

vanity: ____something worthless, trivial, or pointless____

Outline:

1. Without God, nothing man does on earth can have meaning or purpose. It is all ____vanity____. (Ecclesiastes 2:12-23)
2. It is God who gives ____meaning____ and ____purpose____ to life and because of this we can enjoy it. (Ecclesiastes 2:24-26; 3:9-15)
3. The best life comes from ____fearing God____ and obeying Him. (Ecclesiastes 8:12-13; 12:13-14)

SONG OF SOLOMON

Author: Solomon

Key Terms:

simile: a figure of speech that compares two unlike things using "like" or "as"

metaphor: a figure of speech that compares two unlike things without using "like" or "as"

Outline:

1. The Song of Solomon (or Song of Songs) is a love poem depicting the importance and beauty of God's gift of marriage.
2. Examples of simile and metaphor: Song of Solomon 2:2; 4:1-3; 5:14

JOB

Author: Unknown

Key Terms:

comfort: a feeling of relief from affliction

Outline:

The book depicts the story of Job, who in the midst of great suffering comes to realize that true comfort only comes from trusting in the wisdom of God. (Job 42:1-6)

Memory Verse:

Proverbs 15:1-2

A soft answer turneth away wrath: but grievous words stir up anger.
The tongue of the wise useth knowledge aright : but the mouth of fools poureth out foolishness.

REVIEW: POETRY AND WISDOM LITERATURE

Facts to Know: Fill in the correct answer associated with description.

rhythm & rhyme	two aspects of poetry
parallelism	aspect of Hebrew poetry that rhymes ideas
David	author of the majority of the Psalms
praise	type of song that praises God for who he is
thanksgiving	type of song that thanks God for answering prayers
lament	type of song that expresses sadness or fear
confidence	type of song that expresses trust in God
kingship	type of song focused on the Davidic Monarchy
wisdom	type of song that reflects wisdom literature
fear of God	the beginning of knowledge
Solomon	author of the majority of Proverbs
Job	man who, while suffering, realized comfort comes from trusting God

Hebrew Parallelism: Fill in the correct type of parallelism associated with each description.

1. The first part makes a statement and the second part repeats the statement in a different way. Synonymous/Repeating
2. The first part makes a statement and the second part tells the opposite of that statement. Antithetic/Opposite
3. The first part makes a statement and the second part completes the idea started by the first. Synthetic/Completing

Vocabulary:

comfort	corporate worship	genre	metaphor
psalm/hymn	simile	vanity	wisdom

psalm/hymn	song of praise to God
corporate worship	all the people of God gathering in worship

genre	a category of artistic work
wisdom	the skill of living in a godly way
vanity	something worthless or pointless
simile	a figure of speech that compares two unlike things using "like" or "as"
metaphor	a figure of speech that compares two unlike things without using "like" or "as"
comfort	a feeling of relief from affliction

Scripture Memorization: Write the Scripture verse from memory. Be accurate.

Psalm 1 Blessed is the man that walketh not in the counsel of the ungodly, nor standeth in the way of sinners, nor sitteth in the seat of the scornful.
But his delight is in the law of the Lord; and in his law doth he meditate day and night.
And he shall be like a tree planted by the rivers of water, that bringeth forth his fruit in his season; his leaf also shall not wither; and whatsoever he doeth shall prosper.
The ungodly are not so; but are like the chaff which the wind driveth away. Therefore the ungodly shall not stand in the judgment, nor sinners in the congregation of the righteous.
For the Lord knoweth the way of the righteous: but the way of the ungodly shall perish.

Proverbs 15:1-2 A soft answer turneth away wrath: but grievous words stir up anger.
The tongue of the wise useth knowledge aright : but the mouth of fools poureth out foolishness.

NEW TESTAMENT

GOSPELS
Matthew
Mark
Luke
John

HISTORY
Acts

PAULINE EPISTLES
Romans
I Corinthians
II Corinthians
Galatians
Ephesians
Philippians
Colossians
I Thessalonians
II Thessalonians
I Timothy
II Timothy
Titus
Philemon

GENERAL EPISTLES
Hebrews
James
I Peter
II Peter
I John
II John
III John
Jude

BOOK OF PROPHECY
Revelation

*Books of the Bible in canonical order

THE INTERTESTAMENTAL PERIOD

Approximately 400 years passed between the return of Nehemiah with the third wave of exiles and the time of Jesus. This period between the Old Testament and the New Testament is known as the **intertestamental period**. The primary sources we have to learn of this period of Jewish history are the Apocrypha (Deuterocanonical Books) and a Jewish historian named Josephus.

Key Terms:

Palestine: the Roman name for Canaan/ the Promised Land

diaspora: spread of Jews all over Roman Empire

synagogue: local place of worship for Jews during the dispersion

Hellenization: the spreading of the Greek culture and way of life

Outline:

Though many Jews returned to Palestine after Babylon was conquered by the Persians, still many Jews were scattered throughout the Persian Empire and remained scattered throughout the land when it was overtaken by the Roman Empire. This event is called the diaspora.

Even with Cyrus aiding the Jews in reconstructing the temple, the Jews had grown accustomed to worshipping in local assemblies called synagogues.

In 330 B.C. Alexander the Great supplanted Persian rule in Jerusalem and promoted Hellenization throughout his kingdom.

After Alexander's death in 323 B.C., his kingdom was split up among his generals. Two major empires were forged: The Syrian Empire ruled by the Seleucids and the Egyptian Empire ruled by the Ptolemies.

The Jews, under the rule of the Ptolemies, were given great freedom and even flourished. A group of Jews in Alexandria, the capital city in Egypt, was even encouraged to translate the Hebrew Bible into the Greek language. This translation was called the Septuagint.

Ever since the division of Alexander's kingdom, the Seleucids and Ptolemies fought over the control of Palestine. In 198 B.C. the Seleucids were successful in occupying Palestine and promoted Hellenization even stronger than the Ptolemies.

The rising influence of Hellenistic culture caused a rift between those Jews willing to accept Greek culture and those who wanted to remain true to the Law of Moses. The group that resisted the Hellenization of Jewish culture was called the ___Hasidim___ ("pious ones").

Eventually the Seleucid King Antiochus IV Epiphanes forced Greek culture upon the Jews by desecrating the ___temple___ and turning it into a temple of ___Zeus___.

An elderly priest named ___Mattathias___ led his family in revolt against Syria in ___167 B.C.___. His son ___Judas Maccabeus___ assumed leadership and continued what would be called the ___Maccabean Revolt___.

In 164 B.C. Judas Maccabeus was able to recapture the temple and rededicate it to God. This event is celebrated by Jews to this day during the "Festival of Lights" or ___Hanukkah___.

The war continued until ___142 B.C.___ when the Maccabeans were finally able to gain independence for Judea. After the close of the war, the Maccabean family ruled in Judea until 63 B.C. This period of rule is known as the ___Hasmonean Dynasty___, named after an ancestor of the Maccabean family.

During the Hasmonean Dynasty, the Jews continued to be divided in terms of their understanding of true Jewish culture. A group a wealthy priests who were greatly influenced by Hellenism established themselves as the High Priests during this period and were called ___Sadducees___. In opposition to the Sadducees, a group of Jewish elders that found its origin in the Hasidim fought to maintain the purity of the Law. These were called ___Pharisees___.

In ___63 B.C.___ Palestine once again lost its independence, this time to ___Pompey___ and the Romans. By 37 B.C. the Hasmonean family had lost all influence in Judea, and Rome gave Herod reign over Palestine.

NEW TESTAMENT

At the time of Jesus the Roman Empire had been fully established. The Romans continued to promote Hellenistic culture, and in Jesus' day the trade language continued to be Greek. The New Testament was written in Hellenistic Greek, which is also referred to as ______Koine Greek______.

Because of Rome's control over the known world, the New Testament period was a time of relative peace. This peace is called the "______Pax Romana______," or the Peace of Rome, and it made it possible for people to travel the roads connecting the vast Empire in safety. This fact provided the perfect setting for the spreading of the gospel throughout the world.

An important theme that is present throughout the New Testament is the concept of "______already, but not yet______." In the Old Testament, God promised that He would save His people from the destructive power of sin and establish a perfect kingdom through the line of David. When Jesus of Nazareth came in fulfilment of these promises the Jews expected all their enemies to be destroyed and a new, eternal kingdom to be established on earth. Jesus' ministry did bring about a new kingdom, but not the way they expected. The enemies of the Jews were not destroyed and no king reigned in Judah. However, through Jesus they received forgiveness of sins and His kingdom grew with every new believer. In Jesus the kingdom was **already** here, but it was **not yet** fully realized.

THE GOSPELS

The Gospels are the four books in the New Testament that depict the life, death, and resurrection of Jesus of Nazareth as fulfilment of the Old Testament promise for a Messiah. They are written as ancient biography, following significant events surrounding the teachings of Jesus. These events take place between 6 B.C. and A.D. 33. Each Gospel is named after the recognized author of the book.

The four Gospels are:

1. Matthew
2. Mark
3. Luke
4. John

Note to Teacher: Read the overviews for all four Gospels in *Christian Studies IV: A Chronological Overview of the Bible* before answering this section.

Despite different backgrounds and times of writing, the messages of the Gospels are essentially the same. Although the four Gospels all basically cover the same events, each author had a particular purpose in the writing of his book:

Matthew was a tax collector before he became a disciple. He primarily writes to Jews, revealing Jesus is the fulfilment of the Old Testament's promise of a __savior__ and demonstrating the Jews' rejection of Him.

Mark was an attendant and writer for Peter. He focuses on the __actions__ and __miracles__ of Jesus to demonstrate His authority as the Son of God.

Luke was a physician, companion of Paul and a historian. Luke's Gospel is part of a two-volume set (including Acts) that is written for a man named __Theophilus__. It is a substantial historical account that is intended to provide certainty in the story and teachings of Jesus.

John was a disciple who regarded himself as the "disciple whom Jesus loved." John emphasizes Jesus as God in human flesh; the __Messiah__ sent by God to provide eternal life.

We call Matthew, Mark, and Luke __Synoptic Gospels__ because they have similar content and style.

Key People:

1. Man who preached repentance and baptized in the Jordan river: John the Baptist
2. Parents of Jesus: Joseph and Mary
3. Roman governor of Judea at the time of Jesus' birth: Herod
4. Followers selected by Jesus: the 12 disciples
5. Religious leaders focused on maintaining the purity of the Law: Pharisees

Key Terms:

gospel: the good news of the salvation provided by Jesus' life, death, and resurrection

Christ: chosen Messiah

kingdom: a domain ruled by a king

salvation: deliverance from the power and penalty of sin

parable: Jesus' method of teaching by using stories

Outline:

1. Jesus is the Word that existed with God from the beginning. (John 1:1-5)
2. Jesus is born as a man in the little town of Bethlehem in 4 B.C.. (Luke 2:1-21)
3. John the Baptist baptizes Jesus, and the Father expresses His pleasure in the Son. (Matt. 3:13-17)
4. Jesus goes into the wilderness for 40 days and is tempted. (Luke 4:1-13)
5. Jesus performs His first miracle at a wedding in Cana by turning water into wine. (John 2:1-11)
6. Jesus gives the Beatitudes during the Sermon on the Mount. (Matt. 5:1-12)
7. Jesus raises Lazarus from the dead, and the Pharisees plot to have Him killed. (John 11:28-54)
8. Jesus cleanses the temple by overthrowing the tables of the money changers, and the Sadducees plot to destroy Him. (Mark 11:15-19)
9. Jesus observes the Passover with His disciples and is betrayed by Judas. (Luke 22:1-23, 39-53)
10. Jesus is condemned by the people and crucified. (Matt. 27:11-55)

11. Jesus is buried but is resurrected on the ______third day______. (Matt. 28:1-15)

12. Jesus tells the disciples to "make disciples of all nations," which is referred to as the ______Great Commission______. (Matt. 28:16-20)

Memory Verses:

Mark 8:34-37

Whosoever will come after me, let him deny himself and take up his cross and follow me. For whosoever will save his life shall lose it; but whosoever shall lose his life for my sake and the gospel's, the same shall save it. For what shall it profit a man, if he shall gain the whole world, and lose his own soul? Or what shall a man give in exchange for his soul?

ACTS

The book of Acts is the second volume of Luke's work for Theophilus. Acts gives an organized record of what has taken place since the resurrection of Jesus; namely the acts of the apostles and the establishment of Christ's Church.

Author: Luke

Time period covered within the book: A.D. 33 - 67

Key People:

1. The disciple who preached at Pentecost: Peter
2. The first Christian martyr: Stephen
3. Witness in Samaria: Philip
4. Pharisee who was confronted by Jesus and made an apostle: Paul

Key Terms:

martyr: one who chooses to suffer death rather than renounce religious beliefs

witness: a person who testifies to events or facts within his own knowledge

apostle: an official messenger of the gospel

Gentile: a person who is not Jewish

Outline:

1. Before Jesus ascended into heaven He promised the disciples that He would give them the Holy Spirit, and they would become His witnesses to Jerusalem, Judea and Samaria, and to the ends of the earth. (Acts 1:1-8)
2. Jesus ascends into heaven and promises His return. (Acts 1:9-11)

The rest of Acts displays how the disciples did as Jesus said and took the gospel to Jerusalem, Judea/Samaria, and the ends of the earth.

Jerusalem:

1. The Spirit was given to the followers of Jesus at __Pentecost__, and the people from many foreign nations heard Peter preach the gospel __in their own language__. (Acts 2:1-21)
2. Stephen is stoned for preaching in Jerusalem. (Acts 7:54-60)

Judea and Samaria:

1. Philip baptizes the __Ethiopian Eunuch__. (Acts 8:26-40)
2. Saul sees Jesus and becomes an __apostle__. (Acts 9:1-22)

The Ends of the Earth:

1. Paul leaves on his first missionary journey preaching the gospel from Palestine to Asia and starting churches in many cities. These include __Antioch__ and the cities in __Galatia__. (Acts 13: 44-52)
2. Paul meets with __Peter__ and __an assembly of believers__ in Jerusalem to discuss Gentiles in the Church. (Acts 15:1-11)
3. Paul leaves on his second missionary journey preaching the gospel all the way to Macedonia. Among the cities in which he starts churches are __Philippi__, __Thessalonica__, __Corinth__, and __Ephesus__. (Acts 16-20)
4. During this journey Paul reasons with the __Athenian men__ in the Areopagus (Mars Hill). (Acts 17:22-34)
5. Paul leaves on his third missionary journey, preaching and teaching, and visiting and encouraging the churches throughout the __Mediterranean__. (Acts 20:2-3)
6. Paul is imprisoned. (Acts 21:27-35)

Memory Verses:

Acts 1:8

But ye shall receive power, after that the Holy Ghost is come upon you: and ye shall be witnesses unto me both in Jerusalem, and in all Judaea, and in Samaria, and unto the uttermost part of the earth.

PAUL'S FIRST AND SECOND JOURNEY

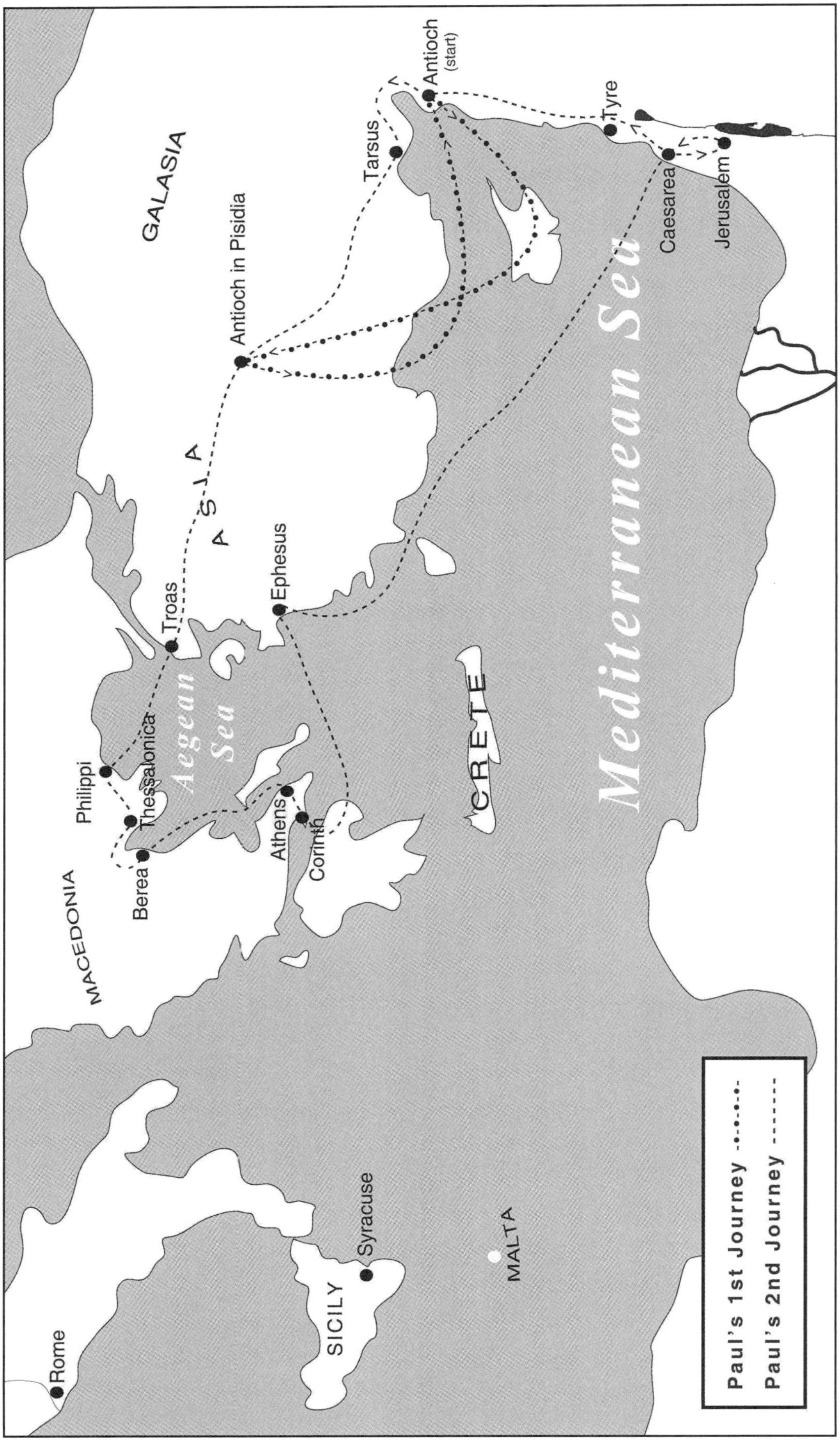

PAUL'S THIRD JOURNEY AND PAUL SENT TO ROME

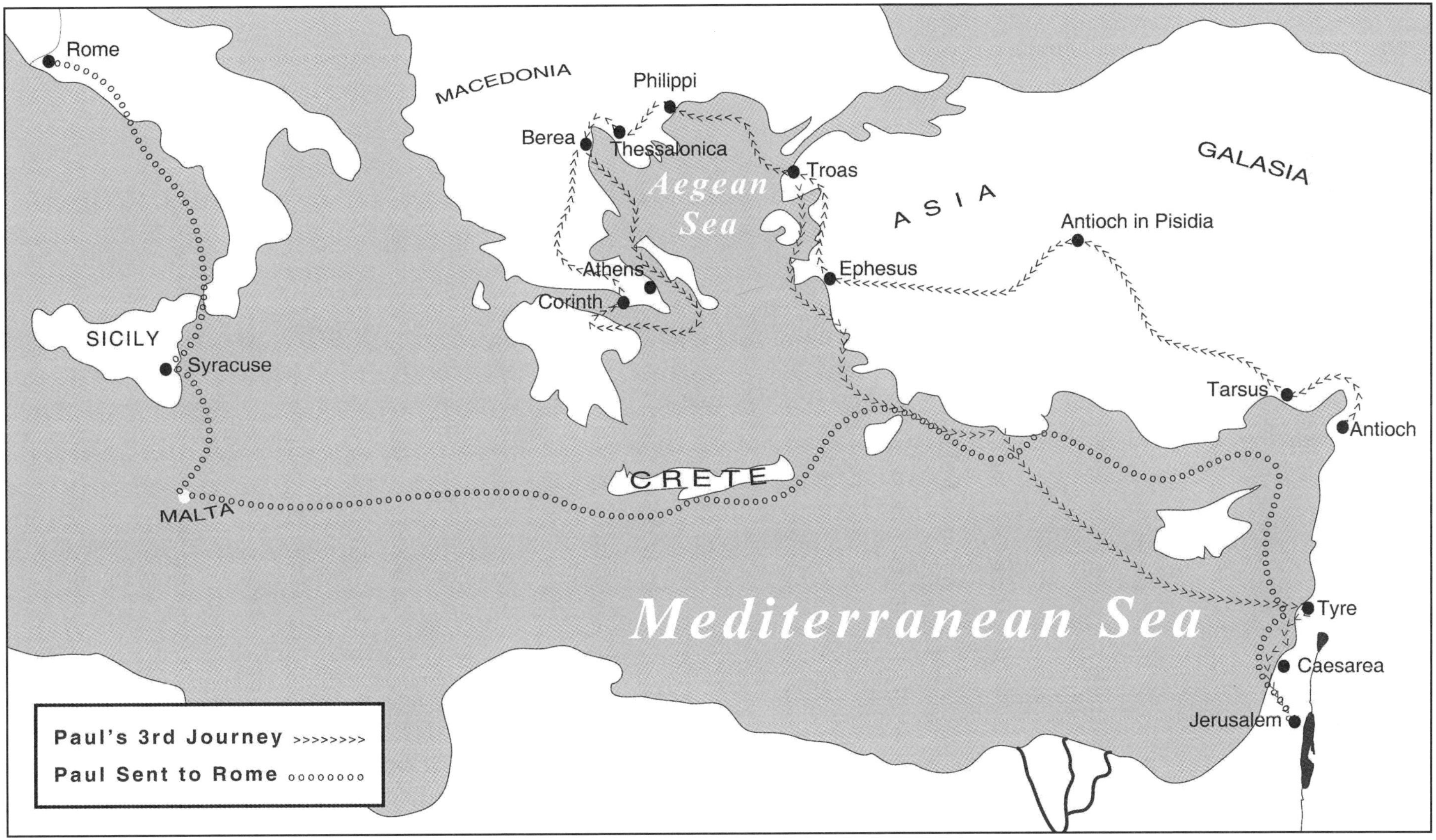

REVIEW: INTERTESTAMENTAL PERIOD - ACTS

Timeline: Fill in the correct date associated with the event.

167-142 B.C.	Maccabean Revolt
63 B.C.	Pompey conquers Palestine
4 B.C.	birth of Christ

Key People: Fill in the correct person associated with the description.

Mattathius	elderly priest who led a revolt against Syria
Judas Maccabeus	recaptured the temple from the Seleucids
Pompey	conquered Palestine for Rome
Matthew	tax collector who became a disciple
Mark	attendant and writer for Peter
Luke	physician and historian
John	"disciple whom Jesus loved"
Theophilus	recipient of Luke's two-volume work
John the Baptist	man who preached repentance and baptized in the Jordan River
Joseph and Mary	parents of Jesus
Herod	Roman governor of Judea at the time of Jesus' birth
12 disciples	followers selected by Jesus
Pharisees	religious leaders focused on maintaining the purity of the Law
Peter	disciple who preached at Pentecost
Stephen	first Christian martyr
Philip	witness in Samaria
Paul	Pharisee who was confronted by Jesus and made an apostle

Facts to Know: Fill in the correct answer associated with the description.

Hasidim	Jewish group that resisted Hellenization; "pious ones"
Hanukkah	Jewish celebration commemorating the recapturing of the temple
Hasmonean Dynasty	rule of the Maccabean family

Sadducees ________ wealthy priests influenced by Hellenism

Pax Romana ________ Peace of Rome

Synoptic Gospels ________ Gospels that have similar content and style

Bethlehem ________ town in which Jesus was born

turning water into wine ________ Jesus' first miracle

Great Commission ________ "make disciples of all nations"

Holy Spirit ________ given by Jesus at Pentecost

Facts to Know: Write in the correct answer.

Important theme present throughout the New Testament: already, but not yet

The disciples became witnesses to Jerusalem, Judea and Samaria, and all the earth

REVIEW: INTERTESTAMENTAL PERIOD - ACTS

Vocabulary:

apostle	Christ	diaspora	Gentile
gospel	Hellenization	kingdom	martyr
Palestine	parable	salvation	synagogue
witness			

Palestine	the Roman name for Canaan
diaspora	spread of Jews all over the Roman Empire
synagogue	local place of worship for Jews during the diaspora
Hellenization	the spreading of the Greek culture and way of life
gospel	the good news of the salvation provided by Jesus' life, death, and resurrection
Christ	chosen Messiah
kingdom	a domain ruled by a king
salvation	deliverance from the power and penalty of sin
parable	Jesus' method of teaching by using stories
martyr	one who chooses to suffer death rather than renounce religious beliefs
witness	a person who testifies to events or facts within his own knowledge
apostle	an official messenger of the gospel
Gentile	a person who is not Jewish

Scripture Memorization: Write the Scripture verse from memory. Be accurate.

Mark 8:34-37 Whosoever will come after me, let him deny himself and take up his cross and follow me. For whosoever will save his life shall lose it; but whosoever shall lose his life for my sake and the gospel's, the same shall save it. For what shall it profit a man, if he shall gain the whole world, and lose his own soul? Or what shall a man give in exchange for his soul?

Acts 1:8 But ye shall receive power, after that the Holy Ghost is come upon you: and ye shall be witnesses unto me both in Jerusalem, and in all Judea, and in Samaria, and unto the uttermost part of the earth.

THE EPISTLES

Twenty-one of the twenty-seven books of the New Testament are epistles, or letters. These letters can be addressed to either (1) a particular church, (2) a group of churches, or (3) an individual person.

The New Testament divides these letters into two sections. The first contains all those epistles written by Paul, called the Pauline Epistles (Romans-Philemon). The second contains all those epistles written by other writers, called the General Epistles (Hebrews-Jude). Within these sections the letters are simply arranged by size.

Though the division of Pauline and General Epistles will be maintained, for the purpose of this course the Epistles will be handled in the order they were composed.

The majority of the Epistles contain three sections. These are as follows:

1. The Opening/Greeting : contains the writer, the recipient, a salutation, and a prayer.
2. The Body : contains the reason for writing and the main portion of content or teaching.
3. The Closing : can contain final instructions, prayer requests, travel plans, and/or a benediction.

THE PAULINE EPISTLES

The Pauline Epistles were written by Paul as a means of instruction and encouragement for the churches throughout the known world—both those he founded and those of which he later learned.

GALATIANS

Recipient: churches in the province of Galatia

Date written & occasion: A.D. 48; written while Paul was in Antioch during his 1st missionary journey

Key Terms:

heresy: false teaching

Outline:

Paul was writing to correct the false idea that to be saved a Gentile would have to become essentially Jewish. Instead, Paul expresses that salvation only comes through faith. (Galatians 3:10-11, 23-29)

I & II THESSALONIANS

Recipient: the church in the city of Thessalonica

Date written & occasion: A.D. 49-51; written while Paul was in Corinth during his 2nd missionary journey

Key Terms:

Second Coming: The time when Jesus will return and judge the world; Day of the Lord

Outline:

I Thessalonians

1. Paul affirms the church in its faith and encourages them to continue to to grow in faith and godliness. (I Thes. 1:2-10)
2. Paul corrects the misunderstanding that those who die will miss the second coming. Both the dead and those living will be taken to be with God when Jesus returns, but it will come suddenly and they must live right before God in the meantime. (I Thes. 4:13-5:11)

II Thessalonians

The people have been told that the Second Coming has already happened, but Paul explains that this is not true and many things must happen before Christ's return. (II Thes. 2:1-12)

I & II CORINTHIANS

Recipient: the church in the city of Corinth

Date written & occasion: A.D. 53-56; I Corinthians was written while Paul was in Ephesus and II Corinthians was written while Paul was in Macedonia, both during his 3rd missionary journey.

Key Terms:

immorality: immoral behavior

division: separation because of different opinions

generosity: readiness or willingness to give

Outline:

I Corinthians

1. The church in Corinth has fallen into many forms of immorality, and Paul reminds them that they should live in the way God commands. (I Cor. 7:17, 10:31-11:1)
2. The church is quarreling over many matters, and Paul urges them to seek unity and community and not fight. (I Cor. 12:12-27)

II Corinthians

Paul is glad that the Corinthians have repented and are no longer living in immorality, but he encourages them to be more generous with what they have. (II Cor. 8:1-15)

Memory Verse

I Corinthians 13:4-8

Love suffereth long, and is kind; love envieth not; love vaunteth not itself, is not puffed up, doth not behave itself unseemly, seeketh not her own, is not easily provoked, thinketh no evil; rejoiceth not in iniquity, but rejoiceth in truth; beareth all things, believeth all things, hopeth all things, endureth all things. Love never faileth.

ROMANS

Recipient: the church in Rome

Date written & occasion: A.D. 57; written while Paul was in Corinth during his 3rd missionary journey

Key Terms:

theology: study of God; understanding of who God is

wrath: God's anger and judgment towards sin

faith: trust in God and His promises

justification: made right with God

grace: the unearned favor and love of God

Outline:

1. Paul writes to the church of Rome to give them a full explanation of his theology.
   (Romans 1:15-17)
2. Paul explains the gospel which expresses that God has wrath towards sin, (Rom. 1:18) but in His grace he sent Jesus to die on the cross, and because of this, man can be justified if he has faith. (Rom. 3:21-23)

EPHESIANS, PHILIPPIANS, COLOSSIANS, PHILEMON

Ephesians, Philippians, Colossians, and Philemon were all written while Paul was under house arrest in Rome. Because of this, these four letters are often referred to as the "Prison Letters."

All four books were written in A.D. 62.

EPHESIANS

Recipient: the church in the city of Ephesus

Key Terms:

reconciliation: to make a friend of an enemy

Outline:

The letter of the Ephesians has basically two parts:

1. First, Paul explains that believing in the gospel reconciles man to God and the rest of mankind. (Eph. 2:12-19)
2. Second, Paul explains how to live because of this reconciliation. (Eph. 4:1-6)

PHILIPPIANS

Recipient: the church in the city of Philippi

Key Terms:

joy: inward hope despite circumstances

humility: considering others more important than yourself

Outline:

Paul tells the Christians in Philippi to look to Jesus as their example of humility in order to live a life of joy even in the face of trials. (Pilippians 2:1-11)

COLOSSIANS

Recipient: the church in the city of ______Colossae______

Outline:

Paul encourages the church to trust in Christ above all other ______rulers______ and ______spiritual forces______. (Colossians 1:15-20)

PHILEMON

Recipient: Christian in the church in the city of ______Colossae______ named ______Philemon______

Outline:

Paul challenges Philemon to see that the gospel makes all men ______equal______ . (Philemon 8-16)

Memory Verse:

Ephesians 2:8-9

For by grace are ye saved through faith; and that not of yourselves: it is the gift of God: Not of works, lest any man should boast.

I & II TIMOTHY AND TITUS

These three letters were written by Paul specifically to leaders within the church to give them further instructions and guidance for dealing with false teachings rising in the church. Because of this, these three letters are often referred to as the " Pastoral Letters ."

Date: A.D. 62-64

I TIMOTHY

Recipient: a coworker of Paul and leader in the church of Ephesus named Timothy

Occasion: I Timothy was written while Paul was doing ministry after being released from house arrest.

Key Terms:

behavior: manner of conducting oneself

Outline:

Paul is instructing Timothy on the godly behavior that should always accompany the true gospel. (I Timothy 3:14-16)

TITUS

Recipient: a coworker of Paul and leader among the churches in Crete named Titus

Occasion: Titus was written while Paul was doing ministry after being released from house arrest.

Key Terms:

leader: one who goes before and directs others

Outline:

Paul reminds Titus of the importance of strong leaders in the church modeling godly living and combatting false teaching. (Titus 1:5-9)

II TIMOTHY

Recipient: Timothy

Occasion: II Timothy was written while Paul was under arrest in Rome for the second time, this time awaiting his execution.

Key Terms:

perseverance: persistence in spite of difficulties

Outline:

Paul encourages Timothy to endure all trials for the sake of the gospel and to persevere in the faith until the end, even as he was nearing the end of his life. (II Timothy 3:14-17; 4:6-7)

Memory Verse:

II Timothy 3:16-17

All scripture is given by inspiration of God, and is profitable for doctrine, for reproof, for correction, for instruction in righteousness: That the man of God may be perfect, thoroughly furnished unto all good works.

THE GENERAL EPISTLES

The remaining letters of the New Testament are written by a collection of authors and are usually addressed to a general audience rather than a specific church or person. These letters were widely circulated (like Paul's letters) among churches throughout the Roman Empire.

JAMES

Author: James, leader in the church in Jerusalem (not the disciple)

Recipient: Jewish Christians in and around Palestine

Date: A.D. 40-45

Key Terms:

evidence: ground for belief or disbelief; proof

Outline:

James writes to make it clear that the evidence for a life changed by the gospel is a life marked by works (good deeds). (James 1:19-24, 2:14-18)

I & II PETER

Author: Peter, the Apostle

Recipient: Churches in the Roman provinces of Asia Minor

Date written & occasion: A.D. 62-67; written during the reign of Nero, Emperor of Rome, while he was persecuting all Christians

Key Terms:

suffering: experiencing pain or distress

persecution: torturing or killing people because of their beliefs

Outline:

I Peter

Peter encourages Christians to look to Christ who suffered on our behalf, in order to endure suffering for His sake. (I Peter 3:8-18)

II Peter

Peter further challenges Christians to live godly lives even in the midst of persecution because of the grace shown to them through Christ. (II Peter 1:5-11)

JUDE

Author: Jude, brother of James

Recipient: Jewish Christians dispersed throughout the Roman Empire

Date written & occasion: A.D. 65; written during the reign of Nero

Outline:

Jude challenges the church to resist false teaching and hold fast to the one true faith. (Jude 17-23)

HEBREWS

Author: Anonymous

Recipient: Jewish Christians in Rome and Palestine

Date written & occasion: before 70 A.D.; written during the reign of Nero

Key Terms:

superiority: greater in quality and worth

Outline:

1. The author goes to great lengths to prove that Jesus and what He has accomplished is superior to all other beings and covenant institutions. (Hebrews 3:1-6)
2. Because Jesus is superior to all things, Christians can have confidence in their salvation and endure to the end. (Hebrews 12:1-2)

Memory Verse:

Hebrews 12:1-2

Wherefore seeing we also are compassed about with so great a cloud of witnesses, let us lay aside every weight, and the sin which doth so easily beset us, and let us run with patience the race that is set before us, looking unto Jesus the author and finisher of our faith; who for the joy that was set before him endured the cross, despising the shame, and is set down at the right hand of the throne of God.

I, II, & III JOHN

Author: John, the Apostle

Recipient: I & II John are written to churches in Ephesus; III John is written to a leader in Ephesus named Gaius.

Date written & occasion: likely between 70-90 A.D; written while in Ephesus during the reign of Domitian

Key Terms:

Gnosticism: an ancient belief that considered all matter to be evil and only the spiritual to be good

propitiation: a sacrifice that bears God's wrath

Outline:

I John

1. John wrote to combat the false teaching of Gnosticism and assure his readers that Jesus came in the flesh. (I John 4:1-6)
2. Because God has shown such great love by sending Jesus as the propitiation for the sins of man, John encourages his readers to love one another. (I John 4:7-21)

II John

John further encourages the churches in Ephesus to love each other like God has loved them and to live according to God's commandments. (II John 4-8)

III John

John encourages his friend Gaius to stay faithful to the truth even in the face of opposition. (III John 5-11)

REVELATION

The book of Revelation is a prime example of Apocalyptic literature. Apocalyptic literature is marked by vivid imagery and visions of future events. Like Daniel and Ezekiel, Revelation contains a lot of symbolic language. Because of the difficulty in understanding the exact meaning of the visions and prophecies described in Revelation, the book has been subject to a variety of interpretations.

Author: John, the Apostle

Recipient: although not considered an epistle, Revelation was written for churches in seven cities of Asia Minor

Date written & occasion: A.D. 95-96; written while John was in exile on the island of Patmos for preaching and prophesying

Key Terms:

apocalypse: a revelation of hidden realities; the end of the world

symbolism: language that uses images instead of direct expression

eschatology: the study of the last things

Outline:

1. In the first section of Revelation John specifically challenges each of the churches not to turn from Christ and adopt the false teachings that surrounded them, for Jesus would soon be returning. (Rev. 1:4-8; 2:24-28; 3:2-3)
2. John goes on to draw a vivid picture of the spiritual battle between Satan and his evil allies, and Christ and His Church. (Rev. 17:7-14)
3. John reveals that in the end Jesus will triumph and defeat sin, death, and Satan. (Rev. 19:11-21)

Memory Verse:

Revelation 21:3-4

And I heard a great voice out of heaven saying, Behold, the tabernacle of God is with men, and he will dwell with them, and they shall be his people, and God himself shall be with them, and be their God. And God shall wipe away all tears from their eyes; and there shall be no more death, neither sorrow, nor crying, neither shall there be any more pain: for the former things are passed away.

REVIEW: THE EPISTLES AND REVELATION

Facts to Know: Fill in the correct answer associated with description.

Pauline Epistles	letters written by Paul
General Epistles	letters written to a general audience
faith	according to Paul, man is justified by ...
Prison Letters	letters written while Paul was under house arrest
Jesus	ultimate example of humility
equal	according to Paul, the gospel makes all men ...
Pastoral Letters	letters of instruction and guidance for leaders
James	leader in the church in Jerusalem
Nero	Emperor of Rome who actively persecuted Christians
John	wrote Revelation while exiled on the island of Patmos

The Epistles and Apocalyptic Literature: Complete the following lists.

The three types of addressees for the epistles:

- a particular church
- a group of churches
- an individual person

The three sections of an epistle:

- Opening/ Greeting
- Body
- Closing

Books Containing Apocalyptic Literature:

- Daniel
- Ezekiel
- Revelation

The Prison Letters:

- Ephesians
- Philippians
- Colossians
- Philemon

The Pastoral Letters:

- I Timothy
- II Timothy
- Titus

Vocabulary:

apocalypse	division	eschatology	evidence
faith	generosity	Gnosticism	grace
heresy	humility	immorality	joy
justification	persecution	perseverance	propitiation
reconciliation	symbolism	theology	wrath

heresy	false teaching
immorality	immoral behavior
division	separation because of different opinions
generosity	readiness and willingness to give
theology	study of God; understanding of who God is
wrath	God's anger and judgment towards sin
faith	trust in God and his promises
justification	made right with God
grace	unearned favor and love of God
reconciliation	to make a friend of an enemy
joy	inward hope despite circumstances
humility	considering others more important than yourself
perseverance	persistence in spite of difficulties
evidence	ground for belief or disbelief; proof
persecution	torturing or killing people because of their beliefs
Gnosticism	ancient belief that considered all matter to be evil and only the spiritual to be good
propitiation	a sacrifice that bears God's wrath
apocalypse	a revelation of hidden realities; the end of the world
symbolism	language that uses images instead of direct expression
eschatology	the study of the last things

REVIEW: THE EPISTLES AND REVELATION

Scripture Memorization: Write the Scripture verse from memory. Be accurate.

I Corinthians 13:4-8 Love suffereth long, and is kind; love envieth not; love vaunteth not itself, is not puffed up, Doth not behave itself unseemly, seeketh not her own, is not easily provoked, thinketh no evil; rejoiceth not in iniquity, but rejoiceth in the truth; beareth all things, believeth all things, hopeth all things, endureth all things. Love never faileth.

Ephesians 2:8-9 For by grace are ye saved through faith; and that not of yourselves: it is the gift of God: Not of works, lest any man should boast.

II Timothy 3:16-17 All scripture is given by inspiration of God, and is profitable for doctrine, for reproof, for correction, for instruction in righteousness: That the man of God may be perfect, thoroughly furnished unto all good works.

Hebrews 12:1-2 Wherefore seeing we also are compassed about with so great a cloud of witnesses, let us lay aside every weight, and the sin which doth so easily beset us, and let us run with patience the race that is set before us, looking unto Jesus the author and finisher of our faith; who for the joy that was set before him endured the cross, despising the shame, and is set down at the right hand of the throne of God.

Revelation 21:3-4 And I heard a great voice out of heaven saying, Behold, the tabernacle of God is with men, and he will dwell with them, and they shall be his people, and God himself shall be with them, and be their God.

And God shall wipe away all tears from their eyes; and there shall be no more death, neither sorrow, nor crying, neither shall there be any more pain: for the former things are passed away.

* Have them review Mark 8:34-37 as well.

CHRISTIAN STUDIES IV

APPENDIX

GENESIS - Scripture Verses

__1:1-5__
In the beginning God created the heaven and the earth. And the earth was without form, and void; and darkness was upon the face of the deep. And the Spirit of God moved upon the face of the waters. And God said, Let there be light: and there was light. And God saw the light, that it was good: and God divided the light from the darkness. And God called the light Day, and the darkness he called Night. And the evening and the morning were the first day.

__1:16__
And God made two great lights; the greater light to rule the day, and the lesser light to rule the night: he made the stars also.

__1:26-28__
And God said, Let us make man in our image, after our likeness; and let them have dominion over the fish of the sea, and over the fowl of the air, and over the cattle, and over all the earth. So God created man in his own image, in the image of God created he him; male and female created he them. And God blessed them, and God said unto them, Be fruitful, and multiply, and replenish the earth, and subdue it.

__1:31__ *And God saw every thing that he had made, and behold, it was very good.*

__2:7__
And the Lord God formed man of the dust of the ground, and breathed into his nostrils the breath of life; and man became a living soul.

__2:8__ *And the Lord God planted a garden eastward in Eden.*

__2:18__ *And the Lord God said, It is not good that man should be alone; I will make a help meet for him.*

__2:23-24__
And Adam said, This is now bone of my bones and flesh of my flesh; she shall be called Woman because she was taken out of Man. Therefore shall a man leave his father and his mother, and shall cleave unto his wife; and they shall be one flesh.

__3:1__ *Now the serpent was more subtle than any beast of the field.*

__3:7-8__ *And they heard the voice of the Lord God walking in the garden in the cool of the day.*

__3:13__ *And the woman said, The serpent beguiled me, and I did eat.*

__3:14-15__
And the Lord God said unto the serpent, Because thou hast done this, thou are cursed above every beast of the field. ... And I will put enmity between thee and the woman, and between thy seed and her seed; it shall bruise thy head, and thou shalt bruise his heel.

__3:20__ *And Adam called his wife's name Eve, because she was the mother of all living.*

__4:2__ *Abel was a keeper of sheep, but Cain was a tiller of the ground.*

4:9 *Am I my brother's keeper?*

6:8-10
But Noah found grace in the eyes of the Lord. Noah was a just man and perfect in his generation, and Noah walked with God. And Noah begat three sons, Shem, Ham, and Japheth.

6:14 *Make thee an ark of gopher wood.*

7:12 *And the rain was upon the earth forty days and forty nights.*

9:13 *I do set my bow in the cloud, and it shall be for a token of a covenant between me and the earth.*

12:1-3
Now the Lord said unto Abram, Get thee out of thy country and from thy kindred and from thy father's house, unto a land that I will show thee; And I will make of thee a great nation and I will bless thee, and in thee shall all families of the earth be blessed. (The Call of Abraham)

13:12 *And Lot pitched his tent toward Sodom.*

17:5 *Thy name shall be called Abraham, for a father of many nations have I made thee.*

19:26 *But Lot's wife looked back, and she became a pillar of salt.*

22:7-8
And Isaac spake unto Abraham his father and said, Behold the fire and the wood: but where is the lamb? And Abraham said, My son, God will provide himself a lamb for a burnt offering.

25:27 *... Esau was a cunning hunter, a man of the field; and Jacob was a plain man dwelling in tents.*

27:22 *The voice is Jacob's voice, but the hands are the hands of Esau.*

29:20 *Jacob served seven years for Rachel and they seemed but a few days, for the love he had to her.*

37:19 *And they said one to another, Behold, this dreamer cometh!*

37:23 *They stripped Joseph out of his coat, his coat of many colors, and they cast him into a pit.*

40:8 *And Joseph said unto them, Do not interpretations belong to God? ...*

41:26 *The seven good kine are seven years; and the seven good ears are seven years; the dream is one.*

45:4, 5, 8
I am Joseph your brother, whom ye sold into Egypt. Now therefore be not grieved with yourselves, for it was not you that sent me hither, but God.

50:25
And Joseph took an oath of the children of Israel saying, God will surely visit you and ye shall carry up my bones from hence.

GENESIS - Drill Questions

1. God's act of bringing the universe into existence (Genesis 1) creation
2. "Out of nothing" (Genesis 1) ex nihilo
3. Latin for "image of God" (Genesis 1:27) imago Dei
4. Where God placed man to enjoy life (Genesis 2) Garden of Eden
5. Tree that God forbade to Adam and Eve (Genesis 2:17) Tree of Knowledge of Good and Evil
6. What God created on the six days of Creation, and what He did on the seventh (Genesis 1-2):
   - day one: matter, light and dark; day and night
   - day two: sky; separated the waters
   - day three: dry land, seas, plants
   - day four: sun, moon, stars
   - day five: animals of seas and air
   - day six: animals and humans
   - day seven: Sabbath, day of rest
7. Most cunning of beasts (Genesis 3) serpent
8. An order of angels (Genesis 3:24) cherubim
9. Adam and Eve's first two sons (Genesis 4) Cain and Abel
10. Adam and Eve's third son (Genesis 4) Seth
11. He built the ark. (Genesis 6-9) Noah
12. How long the rain lasted (Genesis 7) 40 days and 40 nights
13. Bird that Noah sent out to find dry land (Genesis 8) dove
14. Symbol of God's covenant with man (Genesis 9) rainbow
15. Where God confused language (Genesis 11) Tower of Babel
16. Abraham's wife (Genesis 12:5) Sarah
17. Abraham's nephew (Genesis 12) Lot
18. Date of the Call of Abraham (Genesis 12) 2000 BC
19. Land given to Abraham as an inheritance (Genesis 12) Canaan
20. Sarah's handmaid, the mother of Ishmael (Genesis 16) Hagar
21. Father of many nations (Genesis 17:5) Abraham
22. Age of Abraham when Isaac was born (Genesis 17:17 & 21:5) 100

23. Age of Sarah when Isaac was born (Genesis 17:17) 90

24. Two wicked cities destroyed by fire and brimstone (Genesis 19) Sodom and Gomorrah

25. She turned to a pillar of salt. (Genesis 19) Lot's wife

26. Who were the Moabites and Ammonites descendants of? (Genesis 19:37-38) Lot

27. "He who laughs" (Genesis 21:3) Isaac

28. Isaac's twin sons (Genesis 25) Jacob and Esau

29. He sold his birthright for a mess of pottage. (Genesis 25) Esau

30. Jacob's dream (Genesis 28) ladder with angels

31. Jacob's two wives (Genesis 29) Leah and Rachel

32. Jacob's beautiful wife (Genesis 29) Rachel

33. Jacob's plain wife (Genesis 29) Leah

34. The two sons of Jacob and Rachel (Genesis 30:24 & 35:24) Joseph and Benjamin

35. Jacob's name was changed to this (Genesis 32 & 35) Israel

36. The three patriarchs (Genesis) Abraham, Isaac, Jacob

37. The three patriarch wives (Genesis) Sarah, Rebekah, Rachel

38. Joseph's youngest brother (Genesis 35) Benjamin

39. Jacob's favorite son (Genesis 37:3) Joseph

40. He had a coat of many colors. (Genesis 37) Joseph

41. Joseph's two dreams (Genesis 37) brothers' sheaves bowed to his sheaf; sun, moon, stars bowed down to him

42. Egyptian who bought Joseph (Genesis 39) Potiphar

43. She lied about Joseph. (Genesis 39) Potiphar's wife

44. Title for the king of Egypt (Genesis 40) Pharaoh

45. Pharaoh's servants in prison with Joseph (Genesis 40) butler and baker

46. Pharaoh's two dreams (Genesis 41) lean and fat cows; withered and fat ears

47. Number of years of plenty and famine (Genesis 41) seven

48. This was found in Benjamin's sack. (Genesis 44) silver cup

49. The part of Egypt Pharaoh gave to Joseph's family (Genesis 47) Goshen

50. Joseph's two sons (Genesis 48) Ephraim and Manasseh

51. Jacob prophesied this tribe would rule the others. (Genesis 49:8) Judah

EXODUS - Scripture Verses

1:8 *Now there arose up a new king over Egypt who knew not Joseph.*

2:3 *And she took for him an ark of bulrushes and daubed it with slime and with pitch.*

3:2 *Behold, the bush burned with fire, and the bush was not consumed.*

3:6 *I am the God of thy father, the God of Abraham, the God of Isaac, and the God of Jacob. And Moses hid his face; for he was afraid to look upon God.*

3:8 *And I am come down to deliver them out of the hand of the Egyptians, and to bring them up out of that land unto a good land and a large, unto a land flowing with milk and honey.*

3:13-14 *And Moses said unto God, Behold, when I come unto the children of Israel and shall say unto them, The God of your fathers has sent me unto you and they shall say unto me, What is his name? What shall I say unto them? And God said unto Moses, I AM THAT I AM; and he said, Thus shalt you say unto the children of Israel, I AM hath sent me unto you.*

5:1 *And Moses told Pharaoh, Let my people go!*

7:3 *And I will harden Pharaoh's heart, and multiply my signs and my wonders in the land of Egypt.*

12:13 *And when I see the blood, I will pass over you, and the plague shall not be upon you to destroy you, when I smite the land of Egypt.*

15:1 *Then sang Moses and the children of Israel: I will sing unto the Lord, for he hath triumphed gloriously, the horse and his rider, hath he thrown into the sea.*

16:4 *Then the Lord said unto Moses, Behold I will rain bread from heaven for you.*

20:1-17 The 10 Commandments
I am the Lord thy God, which have brought thee out of the land of Egypt, out of the house of bondage.
Thou shalt have no other gods before Me.
Thou shalt not make unto thee any graven image.
Thou shalt not take the name of the Lord thy God in vain.
Remember the Sabbath day, to keep it holy.
Honor thy father and thy mother.
Thou shalt not kill.
Thou shalt not commit adultery.
Thou shalt not steal.
Thou shalt not bear false witness against thy neighbor.
Thou shalt not covet thy neighbor's house, thy neighbor's wife, nor anything that is thy neighbor's.

23:20 *Behold, I send an Angel before thee, to keep thee in the way, and to bring thee into the place which I have prepared.*

31:18 *And he gave unto Moses upon Mount Sinai two tablets of stone, written with the finger of God.*

32:9 *And the Lord said unto Moses, I have seen this people, and behold it is a stiff-necked people.*

EXODUS - Drill Questions

1. The great river of Egypt (Exodus) Nile
2. The direction in which it flows (Exodus) South to North
3. The sea it empties into (Exodus) Mediterranean
4. Two cities built for Pharaoh by the children of Israel (Exodus 1:11) Pithom and Rameses
5. He was hidden in a basket on the Nile. (Exodus 2) Moses
6. After killing an Egyptian, Moses fled here (Exodus 2) Midian
7. The tribe of Moses and Aaron (Exodus 2:1-2 & 4:14) Levi
8. Moses' father-in-law (Exodus 3:1) Jethro
9. How the angel of the Lord appeared to Moses on Mt. Horeb (Exodus 3) a burning bush
10. The Hebrew name for God (Exodus 3) Yahweh
11. The meaning of the Hebrew name for God (Exodus 3) "I am"
12. Moses' brother (Exodus 4) Aaron
13. Bread without yeast (Exodus 12:14-20) unleavened bread
14. The Israelites ate this with their lamb for the Passover. (Exodus 12:8) unleavened bread & bitter herbs
15. Feast celebrating the Exodus from Egypt (Exodus 12:24-28) Passover
16. The departure of Israel from Egypt in 1400 B.C. (Exodus 14) Exodus
17. The great miracle God performed in the Exodus (Exodus 14) parting of Red Sea
18. Moses' sister (Exodus 15) Miriam
19. What the children of Israel always did when difficulties arose (Exodus 15:24 & 16:2) murmur
20. The place of bitter waters in the Wilderness of Shur (Exodus 15) Marah
21. Bread that rained from heaven in the desert (Exodus 16) manna
22. How Moses got water for the Israelites in Massah (Exodus 17) by striking a rock
23. The Israelites defeated these people on the way to Mt. Sinai. (Exodus 17) Amalekites
24. He defeated these people when Moses held up his hands. (Exodus 17) Joshua
25. Mountain where God gave the Law and Ten Commandments (Exodus 19-20 & 34) Mt. Sinai
26. Day of rest (Exodus 20:8-11) Sabbath

27. He spoke with God face to face. (Exodus 24) Moses

28. Number of days Moses was on Mt. Sinai (Exodus 24) 40 days

29. Throne of pure gold on top of the Ark of the Covenant (Exodus 25:17) mercy seat

30. Figures at either end of the mercy seat (Exodus 25:18-20)
golden angels with wings outspread

31. Twelve sacred loaves placed in the Tabernacle each Sabbath (Exodus 25:30 & 35:13)
showbread

32. Seven-branch golden lampstand in the Tabernacle (Exodus 25:31-40 & 37:17-24) Menorah

33. Tent which served as a portable sanctuary for Israel (Exodus 26 & 36) Tabernacle

34. Idol made by the children of Israel while Moses was on Mt. Sinai (Exodus 32) golden calf

35. The tribe the Israelite priests came from (Exodus 40:12-15) Levi

36. The arc of land stretching from the Persian Gulf to Egypt (Exodus) Fertile Crescent

37. The two bodies of water on either side of the Sinai Peninsula (Exodus)
Gulf of Suez, Gulf of Aqaba

38. Four names for God's people (Exodus)
Israelites, Hebrews, Children of Israel, the Chosen People

39. This river empties into the Dead Sea. (Exodus) Jordan River

40. The major river in the Holy Land (Exodus) Jordan River

NUMBERS - Scripture Verses

6:24-26
The Lord bless thee and keep thee: The Lord make his face shine upon thee and be gracious unto thee: The Lord lift up his countenance upon thee and give thee peace. Numbers

14:2 *And all the children of Israel murmured against Moses and against Aaron.*

24:5, 17
How goodly are your tents, O Jacob, and your Tabernacles, O Israel! ... There shall come a Star out of Jacob, and a Scepter shall rise out of Israel ...

DEUTERONOMY - Scripture Verses

30:19
I have set before you life and death, blessing and cursing; therefore choose life, that both thou and thy seed may live.

LEVITICUS, NUMBERS, & DEUTERONOMY - Drill Questions

1. The Promised Land is called a land of (Leviticus 20:24) milk and honey
2. Sacred object that held the Law and Commandments and went before the Israelites on their journeys (Numbers 10:33-35) Ark of the Covenant
3. The two faithful spies (Numbers 14) Joshua and Caleb
4. Because of their sins, the Israelites wandered in the wilderness for (Numbers 14:29-35) 40 years
5. Who said, "There are giants in the land!"? (Numbers 13:31-33) the faithless spies
6. The descendants of Esau who refused to give passage to the Israelites (Numbers 20) Edomites
7. Aaron's son (Numbers 20:22-29) Eleazar
8. God sent fierce snakes to punish the children of Israel, but if they looked on this they would be healed. (Numbers 21) brass serpent on a pole
9. Balak, the king of Moab, called upon this man to curse the Israelites. (Numbers 22) Balaam
10. It spoke to its master after being beaten three times. (Numbers 22) Balaam's donkey
11. God caused him to give a blessing instead of a curse. (Numbers 22-24) Balaam
12. Israel defeated these two peoples before entering the Promised Land. (Deuteronomy 2-3) Amorites & Og, king of Bashan
13. He died on Mt. Nebo without entering the Promised Land. (Deuteronomy 34) Moses
14. Age when he died (Deuteronomy 34:7) 120 years

JOSHUA - Scripture Verses

1:9
Have not I commanded thee? Be strong and of a good courage; be not afraid, neither be thou dismayed: for the Lord thy God is with thee whithersoever thou goest.

10:12 *Sun, stand thou still upon Gibeon and thou, Moon, in the valley of Ajalon.*

JUDGES - Scripture Verses

6:1
And the children of Israel did evil in the sight of the Lord: and the Lord delivered them into the hand of Midian seven years.

21:25 *In those days there was no king in Israel: every man did that which was right in his own eyes.*

RUTH - Scripture Verses

1:16
And Ruth said, Entreat me not to leave thee, or to return from following after thee; for whither thou goest, I will go, and where thou lodgest I will lodge: thy people shall be my people, and thy God, my God.

JOSHUA, JUDGES, & RUTH - Drill Questions

1. He followed Moses as leader of the Israelites. (Joshua 1) Joshua
2. She hid spies in Jericho. (Joshua 2 & 6) Rahab the harlot
3. The river Israel crossed to enter the Promised Land (Joshua 3) Jordan
4. Where the sun stood still (Joshua 9-10) Gibeon
5. She prophesied the defeat of Sisera. (Judges 4-5) Deborah
6. He defeated the Midianites with 300 men. (Judges 6-8) Gideon
7. Gideon's good son that told the parable of the bramble (Judges 9) Jotham
8. Wicked judge that killed 70 of his brothers, save Jotham (Judges 9) Abimelech
9. They ruled Israel between Joshua and the Kings. the Judges
10. He made a rash vow and sacrificed his own daughter. (Judges 11) Jephthah
11. Enemies of Israel that lived on the seacoast of Canaan (Judges 13) Philistines
12. The strongest man in the Bible (Judges 13-16) Samson
13. He killed 1,000 Philistines with this. (Judges 15) the jawbone of a donkey
14. The source of his great strength (Judges 16) his hair
15. She betrayed him to the Philistines. (Judges 16) Delilah
16. The four major judges (Judges) Deborah, Gideon, Jephthah, Samson
17. Faithful daughter-in-law to Naomi (Ruth 1) Ruth
18. The great-grandfather of King David (Ruth 2) Boaz
19. Four names for Canaan Promised Land, Israel, Palestine, Holy Land
20. Two books of the Bible named for women Ruth and Esther

I SAMUEL - Scripture Verses

3:19-20
And Samuel grew, and the Lord was with him, and let none of his words fall to the ground. And all Israel from Dan even to Beersheba knew that Samuel was established to be a prophet of the Lord.

16:7 *For the Lord seeth not as man seeth; for man looketh on the outward appearance, but the Lord looketh on the heart.*

17:26 *Who is this uncircumcised Philistine that he should defy the armies of the living God?*

17:40 *And he took his staff in his hand, and chose him five smooth stones ... and his sling was in his hand: and he drew near to the Philistine.*

17:45-46
Then David said to the Philistine, Thou comest to me with a sword, and with a spear, and with a shield: but I come to thee in the name of the Lord of hosts. ... This day will the Lord deliver thee into mine hand; and I will smite thee ... that all the earth may know that there is a God in Israel.

18:7
And the women answered one another as they played and said, Saul hath slain his thousands, and David his ten thousands.

II SAMUEL - Scripture Verses

1:19-20
The beauty of Israel is slain upon the high places: how are the mighty fallen!
Tell it not in Gath, publish it not in the streets of Askelon; lest the daughters of the Philistines rejoice, lest the daughters of the uncircumcised triumph.

18:33 *O my son Absalom, my son, my son Absalom! would God I had died for thee, O Absalom, my son, my son!*

23:1 *David, the son of Jesse, the anointed of God, the sweet psalmist of Israel*

I & II SAMUEL - Drill Questions

1. She pledged to give her child to the service of the Lord. (I Samuel 1) Hannah
2. The prayer of Samuel's mother (I Samuel 2) Hannah's Song
3. This priest of Shiloh had corrupt sons. (I Samuel 2) Eli
4. The last judge and a great prophet of God (I Samuel 3) Samuel
5. The elders of Israel wanted a king like (I Samuel 8) "all the other nations"
6. The son of Kish from the Tribe of Benjamin (I Samuel 9) Saul

7. The people's choice of king for Israel (I Samuel 9) Saul

8. A man after God's "own heart" (I Samuel 13:13-14) David

9. The son of Jesse from the Tribe of Judah (I Samuel 16) David

10. City where Samuel found the shepherd boy to be king of Israel (I Samuel 16) Bethlehem

11. Instrument David played to soothe Saul (I Samuel 16) harp

12. The Philistine giant that insulted Israel's God (I Samuel 17) Goliath

13. David's eldest brother that told him to go home (I Samuel 17) Eliab

14. David's weapon of choice against the giant Philistine (I Samuel 17) a stone and a sling

15. David's first wife and the daughter of Saul (I Samuel 18) Michal

16. Saul's son and David's best friend (I Samuel 18-20) Jonathan

17. The number of times that David spared Saul's life (I Samuel 24 & 26) twice

18. The wise lady of Carmel that became David's second wife (I Samuel 25) Abigail

19. The general of Saul's army (I Samuel 26) Abner

20. He told Saul that he and his sons would die in battle. (I Samuel 28) the spirit of Samuel

21. The year David's reign as king of Israel began (II Samuel 5) 1000 BC

22. Sacred object David brought to Jerusalem (II Samuel 6) Ark of the Covenant

23. She despised David's celebrations and dancing. (II Samuel 6) Michal

24. God promised this to David with a covenant. (II Samuel 7:16) an eternal throne

25. God's prophet to David (II Samuel 7 & 12) Nathan

26. The descendants of David (II Samuel 7:11-16) the house of David

27. Jonathan's lame son (II Samuel 9) Mephibosheth

28. When the men went out to battle, David still tarried here. (II Samuel 11:1) Jerusalem

29. The wife that David took from Uriah (II Samuel 11) Bathsheba

30. The general of David's army (II Samuel 11) Joab

31. He told David a parable about a rich man and a poor man. (II Samuel 12) Nathan

32. David's son that led a revolt against his father (II Samuel 15-17) Absalom

33. This enemy of David's was caught in a tree and stabbed to death. (II Samuel 18)

Absalom

I KINGS - Scripture Verses

10:1
And when the queen of Sheba heard of the fame of Solomon concerning the name of the Lord, she came to prove him with hard questions.

19:11-12
But the Lord was not in the wind: and after the wind an earthquake; but the Lord was not in the earthquake. And after the earthquake a fire; but the Lord was not in the fire: and after the fire a still, small voice.

II KINGS - Scripture Verses

2:11 *There appeared a chariot of fire and horses of fire, and Elijah went up by a whirlwind into heaven.*

I & II KINGS - Drill Questions

1. David's son that inherited the throne (I Kings 1-2) Solomon
2. This made Solomon world famous. (I Kings 3 & 4:29-34) his great wisdom
3. The center of Israel's worship (I Kings 6) the temple
4. She brought Solomon questions and gifts from a distant land. (I Kings 10) Queen of Sheba
5. Three kings of Israel's united kingdom (I Kings) Saul, David, Solomon
6. Date the kingdom of Israel divided between North and South (I Kings 12:20) 931 B.C.
7. The Northern Kingdom (I Kings 12:20) Israel
8. He was given control of the Northern Kingdom. (I Kings 12:20) Jeroboam
9. The Southern Kingdom (I Kings 12:20-24) Judah
10. He ruled the Southern Kingdom. (I Kings 12:20-24) Rehoboam
11. God's prophet to Jeroboam (I Kings 11:29-39 & 14:1-18) Ahijah
12. God's prophet that called for famine on Israel because of Ahab's sin (I Kings 16:29-17:1)
    Elijah
13. The wicked, pagan wife of King Ahab of Israel (I Kings 16:31 & 21:23-24, II Kings 9:30-37)
    Jezebel
14. He was murdered by royalty for his vineyard. (I Kings 21) Naboth
15. Elijah rode this to heaven so he never saw death. (II Kings 2) chariot of fire

16. He took the place of Elijah and saw his ascension to heaven. (II Kings 2) Elisha

17. Under Elisha's instructions, he washed himself clean of leprosy in the Jordan. (II Kings 5) Naaman

18. He was the selfish servant of Elisha that got leprosy. (II Kings 5) Gehazi

19. This king set to punishing Ahab's family line. (II Kings 9:6-10) Jehu

20. Queen of Judah for seven years after killing her family rivals (II Kings 11) Athaliah

21. King of Judah that was hidden in the temple as a child (II Kings 11) Joash

22. High priest that protected the child king from Athalia (II Kings 11) Jehoiada

23. The year the Northern Kingdom fell (II Kings 18) 722 B.C.

24. The nation that conquered Israel (II Kings 18:9-12) Assyria

25. Good king who reformed Judah according to the Book of the Law (II Kings 23) Josiah

26. The nation that took the best people and possessions of Jerusalem captive (II Kings 24) Babylon

27. The king of Babylon that brought about Judah's exile (II Kings 24) Nebuchadnezzer

1:8

And the Lord said unto Satan, Hath thou considered my servant Job, that there is none like him in the earth a perfect and upright man, one that feared God, and eschewed evil?

1:21

Naked came I out of my mother's womb, and naked shall I return thither: the Lord giveth, and the Lord taketh away; blessed be the name of the Lord.

2:9

Curse God and die.

14:1-2

Man that is born of a woman is of few days, and full of trouble. He cometh forth like a flower, and is cut down: he fleeth also as a shadow, and continueth not.

16:2

Miserable comforters are ye all.

38:1-7; 39:31-32, 34; 39:9-10, 19-22, 25

Then the Lord answered Job out of the whirlwind, and said, Who is this that darkeneth counsel by words without knowledge? Gird up thy loins like a man; for I will demand of thee and answer thou me. Where wast thou when I laid the foundations of the earth? Declare, if thou hast understanding. Who hath laid the measures thereof, if thou knowest? Or who hath stretched the line upon it? When the morning stars sang together, and all the sons of God shouted for joy? Canst thou bind the sweet influences of Pleiades, or loose the bands of Orion? Canst thou bring forth Mazzaroth in his season? Or canst thou guide Arcturus with his sons? Canst thou lift up thy voice to the clouds, that abundance of waters may cover thee? Will the unicorn be willing to serve thee, or abide by thy crib? Canst thou bind the unicorn with his band in the furrow? Or will he harrow the valleys after thee? Hast thou given the horse strength? Hast thou clothed his neck with thunder? Canst thou make him afraid as a grasshopper? The glory of his nostrils is terrible. He paweth in the valley, and rejoiceth in his strength: he goeth on to meet the armed men. He mocketh at fear, and is not affrighted; neither turneth he back from the sword. He saith among the trumpets, Ha, ha; and he smelleth the battle afar off, the thunder of the captains and the shouting.

39:26-27; 40:15, 17, 19; 41:1-2

Doth the hawk fly by thy wisdom, and stretch her wings toward the south? Doth the eagle mount up at thy command, and make her nest on high? Behold now Behemoth, which I made with thee; he eateth grass as an ox. He moveth his tail like a cedar. He is the chief of the ways of God. Canst thou draw out leviathan with a hook? Or his tongue with a cord, which thou letteth down? Shall he that contendeth with the Almighty instruct him? He that reproveth God let him answer it.

40:3-4; 42:2-3, 5-6

Then Job answered the Lord and said, Behold, I am vile; what shall I answer thee? I will lay mine hand upon my mouth. I know that thou canst do every thing, and that no thought can be withholden from thee. Wherefore have I uttered that I understood not; things too wonderful for me, which I knew not. I have heard of thee by the hearing of the ear: but now mine eye seeth thee. Wherefore I abhor myself, and repent in dust and ashes.

42:12

So the Lord blessed the latter end of Job more than his beginning.

PSALMS - Scripture Verses

1

Blessed is the man that walketh not in the counsel of the ungodly, nor standeth in the way of sinners, nor sitteth in the seat of the scornful.
But his delight is in the law of the Lord; and in his law doth he meditate day and night. And he shall be like a tree planted by the rivers of water, that bringeth forth his fruit in his season; his leaf also shall not wither; and whatsoever he doeth shall prosper.
The ungodly are not so; but are like the chaff which the wind driveth away.
Therefore the ungodly shall not stand in the judgment, nor sinners in the congregation of the righteous.
For the Lord knoweth the way of the righteous: but the way of the ungodly shall perish.

19:1-3 *The heavens declare the glory of God, the firmament showeth his handiwork. Day unto day uttereth speech, night unto night showeth knowledge. There is no speech or language where their voice is not heard.*

23

The Lord is my shepherd; I shall not want. He maketh me to lie down in green pastures: he leadeth me beside the still waters. He restoreth my soul: he leadeth me in the paths of righteousness for his name's sake. Yea, though I walk through the valley of the shadow of death, I will fear no evil: for thou art with me; thy rod and thy staff they comfort me. Thou preparest a table before me in the presence of mine enemies: thou anointest my head with oil; my cup runneth over. Surely goodness and mercy shall follow me all the days of my life: and I will dwell in the house of the Lord forever.

100

Make a joyful noise unto the Lord, all ye lands. Serve the Lord with gladness; come before His presence with singing. Know ye that the Lord, He is God; it is He that hath made us, and not we ourselves; we are His people, and the sheep of His pasture. Enter into His gates with thanksgiving, and into His courts with praise; be thankful unto Him, and bless His name. For the Lord is good; His mercy is everlasting; and His Truth endureth to all generations.

121

I will lift up mine eyes unto the hills, from whence cometh my help.
My help cometh from the Lord, which made heaven and earth.
He will not suffer thy foot to be moved: he that keepeth thee will not slumber.
Behold, he that keepeth Israel shall neither slumber nor sleep.
The Lord is thy keeper: the Lord is thy shade upon thy right hand.
The sun shall not smite thee by day nor the moon by night.
The Lord shall preserve thee from all evil: he shall preserve thy soul.
The Lord shall preserve thy going out and thy coming in from this time forth, and even for evermore.

122:1, 2, 6 *I was glad when they said unto me, Let us go into the house of the Lord.*
Our feet shall stand within thy gates, O Jerusalem.
Pray for the peace of Jerusalem: they shall prosper that love thee.

137:1-4 *By the rivers of Babylon, there we sat down, yea, we wept, when we remembered Zion. We hanged our harps upon the willows in the midst thereof. For there they that carried us away captive required of us a song; and they that wasted us required of us mirth, saying, Sing us one of the songs of Zion. How shall we sing the Lord's song in a strange land?*

PROVERBS - Scripture Verses

15:1 *A soft answer turneth away wrath.*

17:22 *A merry heart doeth good like medicine.*

25:11 *A word fitly spoken is like apples of gold in pictures of silver*

SONG OF SOLOMON - Scripture Verses

2:1 *I am the rose of Sharon, and the lily of the valleys.*

THE PROPHETS - Scripture Verses

Ezra 7:27 *Blessed be the Lord God of our fathers, which hath put such a thing as this in the king's heart, to beautify the house of the Lord which is in Jerusalem.*

Isaiah 7:14 *Behold, a virgin shall conceive and bear a son, and shall call his name Immanuel.*

Isaiah 9:2, 6
The people that walked in darkness have seen a great light. For unto us a child is born, unto us a son is given: and the government shall be upon his shoulder; and his name shall be called Wonderful, Counsellor, The mighty God, The everlasting Father, The Prince of Peace.

Jeremiah 31:31-33
Behold, the days come, saith the Lord, that I will make a new covenant with the house of Israel and with the house of Judah: Not according to the covenant that I made with their fathers ... which my covenant they break ... but I will put my law in their inward parts, and write it in their hearts; and I will be their God, and they shall be my people.

Daniel 5:25-28
And this was the writing that was written, MENE, MENE, TEKEL, UPHARSIN. This is the interpretation of the thing: MENE; God hath numbered thy kingdom, and finished it. TEKEL; Thou art weighed in the balances, and art found wanting. PERES; Thy kingdom is divided and given to the Medes and Persians.

Daniel 6:23 *So Daniel was taken up out of the den, and no manner of hurt was found upon him, because he believed in his God.*

Micah 6:8 *What doth the Lord require of thee, but to do justly, and to love mercy, and to walk humbly with thy God?*

PSALMS & PROPHETS - Drill Questions

1. The year the first exiles returned to Jerusalem (Ezra 1) 536 B.C.
2. Persian king who released Ezra and Nehemiah to rebuild the walls of Jerusalem (Ezra 7) Artaxerxes
3. The scribe and priest that restored the law again (Ezra 7) Ezra
4. Ezra read this to the people in the land. (Ezra 7) the Law of Moses
5. Royal cupbearer who oversaw the reconstruction of Jerusalem's walls (Nehemiah 1-2) Nehemiah
6. Greatest prophet, preacher, statesman, and advisor of Judah Isaiah
7. Great prophet that foresaw both God's judgment and restoration Isaiah
8. The seraphim sang this in Isaiah's vision. (Isaiah 6:3) "Holy, Holy, Holy is the Lord of hosts"
9. The king who received a sign from Isaiah about the coming Messiah (Isaiah 7) Ahaz
10. The five names for the Messiah child (Isaiah 9) Wonderful, Counselor, Mighty God, Everlasting Father, Prince of Peace
11. The Messiah child born to a virgin (Isaiah 9) Jesus Christ
12. He prophesied in Judah during the fall of Jerusalem. (Jeremiah 1) Jeremiah
13. Priest who prophesied for God to the exiles in Babylon (Ezekiel 1-2) Ezekiel
14. Hebrew children thrown in the fiery furnace (Daniel 3) Shadrach, Meshach, Abednego
15. He could read the writing on Babylon's wall. (Daniel 5) Daniel
16. God judged this king with the words "Mene, Mene, Tekel, Upharsin." (Daniel 5) Belshazzar
17. The next great empire after Babylon (Daniel 5:28-31) Medes and Persians
18. He survived the lions' den. (Daniel 6) Daniel
19. Median king who decreed that everyone should respect Daniel's God (Daniel 6) Darius
20. Prophet of Israel that held out hope for God's mercy (Hosea 14) Hosea
21. The first prophet to foretell the fall of Israel and Judah (Amos 2) Amos
22. Unwilling prophet of God to the Ninevites (Jonah 1) Jonah
23. "And Jonah was in the belly of the fish" how long? (Jonah 1:17) three days & three nights
24. "In the days to come, the nations will make plowshares of their ____________ ." (Micah 4:3) swords

MATTHEW, MARK, LUKE, & JOHN - Scripture Verses

Luke 1:46-55
And Mary said, My soul doth magnify the Lord and my spirit rejoices in God my Savior. For He hath regarded the low estate of his handmaiden: for behold, from henceforth all generations shall call me blessed. For he that is mighty hath done great things for me and holy is his name. And his mercy is on them that fear him from generation to generation. He hath shown strength with his arm; he hath scattered the proud in the imagination of their hearts. He hath put down the mighty from their seats, and exalted them of low degree. He hath filled the hungry with good things, and the rich he hath sent empty away. He hath helped his servant Israel, in remembrance of his mercy; as he spake to our fathers, to Abraham and to his seed forever.

Luke 2:7
And she brought forth her firstborn son, and wrapped him in swaddling clothes, and laid him in a manger; because there was no room for them in the inn.

Luke 2:8-11
There were in the same country shepherds abiding in the field, keeping watch over their flock by night. And lo, the angel of the Lord came upon them, and the glory of the Lord shone round about them, and they were sore afraid. And the angel said unto them, Fear not, for behold, I bring you good tidings of great joy, which shall be to all people. For unto you is born this day in the city of David a Savior, who is Christ the Lord.

Luke 2:14 *Glory to God in the highest and on earth peace, good will toward men.*

Matthew 2:1-2
Now when Jesus was born in Bethlehem of Judea in the days of Herod the king, behold, there came wise men from the east to Jerusalem, Saying, Where is he that is born King of the Jews? For we have seen his star in the east, and are come to worship him

Matthew 2:11
They saw the young child with Mary his mother, and fell down, and worshipped him: and when they had opened their treasures, they presented unto him gifts; gold, and frankincense, and myrrh.

Matthew 4:4,7,10
It is written, Man shall not live by bread alone, but by every word that proceedeth out of the mouth of God.
It is written again, Thou shalt not tempt the Lord thy God.
Get thee hence, Satan: for it is written, Thou shalt worship the Lord thy God, and him only shalt thou serve.

Matthew 5:3-12 The Beatitudes
Blessed are the poor in spirit for theirs is the kingdom of heaven. Blessed are they that mourn for they shall be comforted. Blessed are the meek for they shall inherit the earth. Blessed are they which hunger and thirst after righteousness for they shall be filled. Blessed are the merciful for they shall obtain mercy. Blessed are the pure in heart for they shall see God. Blessed are the peacemakers for they shall be called the children of God. Blessed are they which are persecuted for righteousness' sake for theirs is the kingdom of heaven. Blessed are you when men shall revile you and persecute you and shall say all manner of evil against you falsely for my sake. Rejoice and be exceeding glad for great is your reward in heaven, for so persecuted they the prophets which were before you.

Matthew 5:14 *You are the light of the world. A city that is set on a hill cannot be hid*

Matthew 6:9-13
Our Father which art in Heaven, Hallowed be thy name. Thy kingdom come. Thy will be done on Earth as it is in Heaven. Give us this day our daily bread. And forgive us our debts, as we forgive our debtors. And lead us not into temptation, but deliver us from evil. For Thine is the kingdom, and the power, and the glory forever. Amen.

Matthew 7:7 *Ask, and it shall be given you; seek and ye shall find; knock and it shall be opened unto you.*

Matthew 7:13-14
Enter in at the narrow gate: For wide is the gate and broad is the way that leadeth to destruction, and many there be which go in there. For narrow is the gate, and narrow is the way which leadeth to life, and few there be that find it.

Matthew 7:20 *By their fruits ye shall know them.*

Matthew 9:12-13
They that are healthy do not need a physician, but they that are sick. Go and learn what this means: I will have mercy, and not sacrifice: for I have not come to call the righteous, but sinners to repentance.

Luke 4:18-19
The Spirit of the Lord is upon me, because he has anointed me to preach the gospel to the poor; he hath sent me to heal the broken-hearted, to preach deliverance to the captives, and recovering of sight to the blind, to set at liberty them that are bruised, to preach the acceptable year of the Lord.

Mark 8:34-37
Whosoever will come after me, let him deny himself and take up his cross and follow me. For whosoever will save his life shall lose it; but whosoever shall lose his life for my sake and the gospel's, the same shall save it. For what shall it profit a man, if he shall gain the whole world, and lose his own soul? Or what shall a man give in exchange for his soul?

Mark 9:35 *If any man desires to be first, the same shall be last of all, and servant of all..*

Matthew 19:30 *Many that are first shall be last; and the last shall be first.*

John 3:16 *For God so loved the world that He gave his only begotten son, that whosoever believeth in him should not perish, but have everlasting life.*

Luke 10:27-28
Thou shalt love the Lord thy God with all thy heart, and with all thy soul, and with all thy strength, and with all thy mind; and thy neighbor as thyself.

John 6:35 *I am the bread of life.*

John 10:11 *I am the good shepherd: the good shepherd gives his life for his sheep*

John 11:25 *I am the resurrection, and the life. He that believeth in me, though he were dead, yet shall he live.*

John 14:6 *I am the way, the truth, and the life. No man cometh unto the Father but by me.*

Mark 10:14 *Suffer the little children to come unto me and forbid them not, for of such is the kingdom of God.*

Matthew 22:21
Render therefore unto Caesar the things which are Caesar's; and unto God the things which are God's.

Matthew 25:35-40
For I was hungry and you gave me food. I was thirsty and you gave me drink. I was a stranger, and you took me in. I was naked and you clothed me. I was sick and you visited me. I was in prison and you came to me. ... Truly I tell you, inasmuch as you have done it to one of the least of these my brethren, you have done it unto me.

Matthew 26:26-28
Jesus took the bread, and blessed it, and broke it, and gave it to the disciples and said, Take, eat; this is my body. And he took the cup, and gave thanks, and gave it to them saying, Drink ye all of it; For this is my blood of the new testament which is shed for many for the remission of sins.

Matthew 26:41 *Watch and pray, that you enter not into temptation: the spirit indeed is willing, but the flesh is weak.*

Luke 22:42 *Father, if thou be willing, remove this cup from me: nevertheless not my will, but thine, be done.*

The Seven Last Words of Christ

Father, forgive them for they know not what they do. (Luke 23:34)
Woman, Behold thy son. Then he said unto the disciple, Behold thy mother. (John 19:26-27)
My God, My God, Why hast thou forsaken me? (Eloi, Eloi, lama sabachthani?) (Matthew 27:46, Mark 15:34)
I thirst. (John 19:28)
Verily, I say unto thee, today shalt thou be with me in paradise. (Luke 23:43)
Father, into Your hands I commend my spirit. (Luke 23:46)
It is finished. (John 19:30)

John 20:29
Because you have seen me, you have believed. Blessed are they that have not seen, and yet have believed.

MATTHEW, MARK, LUKE, & JOHN - Drill Questions

1. He was struck mute for his disbelief. (Luke 1:18-23) Zacharias
2. The angel of the Annunciation (Luke 1:26-38) Gabriel
3. The angel foretold that John the Baptist would be (Luke 1:11-17) the Highest Prophet of the Lord
4. Mary's cousin and the mother of John (Luke 1:39-45) Elisabeth
5. "My soul doth magnify the Lord and my spirit rejoices in God my Savior." (Luke 1:46-55) Magnificat
6. Jesus' earthly father (Matthew 1:18-25) Joseph
7. He decreed a census at the time of Jesus' birth. (Luke 2:1-3) Caesar Augustus
8. City of David where Jesus was born (Luke 2:4-7) Bethlehem
9. Roman governor of Judea at the time of Jesus' birth (Matthew 2:13-18) Herod
10. Wise Men came from here. (Matthew 2:1-12) Far East
11. Kingly gifts given by the Wise Men (Matthew 2:11) gold, frankincense, and myrrh
12. By an angel, God sent Joseph and the family here. (Matthew 2:13-15) Egypt
13. Town where Jesus grew up (Matthew 2:19-23) Nazareth
14. He preached repentance and baptized in the Jordan River. (Matthew 3:1-6, Mark 1:1-6, Luke 3:1-6, John 1:15-27) John the Baptist
15. How long was Jesus tempted in the wilderness? (Matthew 4:1-11, Mark 1:12-13, Luke 4:1-13) 40 days
16. Jesus' first miracle at a wedding party (John 2:1-11) turning water to wine
17. Where Jesus began His preaching (Matthew 4:12-17, Mark 1:14-15, Luke 4:14-15) Capernaum
18. He went when he heard the words "Follow me." (Matthew 9:9, Mark 2:14, Luke 5:27-28) Matthew
19. The collection of Jesus' ethical teachings (Matthew 5-7) Sermon on the Mount
20. "Our Father which art in heaven, Hallowed be thy name ..." (Matthew 6:9-15, Luke 11:2-4) the Lord's Prayer
21. "Whatever you want that men should do to you, do so to them." (Matthew 7:12) Golden Rule

22. He had faith greater than Jesus had found in all Israel (Matthew 8:5-13, Luke 7:1-10)

Roman centurion

23. Where Jesus raised the widow's dead son (Luke 7:11-17) Nain

24. To whom did Jesus say, "Go and sin no more"? (John 8:1-11) the woman caught in sin

25. The Pharisees accused Jesus of casting out demons in the power of whom? (Matthew 12:22-24, Mark 3:23-30, Luke 11:17-23) Beelzebub

26. To blaspheme the Holy Spirit is to commit what? (Matthew 12:30-32, Mark 3:28-29, Luke 12:10)

the unforgivable sin

27. The sign that Jesus would give the scribes and Pharisees (Matthew 12:38-42, Luke 11:29-32)

the Sign of Jonah

28. Jesus cast seven evil spirits out of her. (Mark 16:9) Mary Magdalene

29. Where is a prophet without honor? (Matthew 13:54-58, Mark 6:1-6, Luke 4:16-30) his home

30. They recognized Jesus wherever He went. (Matthew 8:28-34, Mark 5:1-20, Luke 8:26-39; also Mark 1:32-34 & Luke 4:40-41) the demons

31. To whom did Jesus say, "Be not afraid. Only believe."? (Matthew 9:18-26, Mark 5:21-43)

Jairus

32. The Great Physician (Matthew 9:10-13) Jesus Christ

33. Jesus fed five thousand with this. (Matthew 14:13-21, Mark 6:30-44, Luke 9:10-17, John 6:1-15)

5 loaves and 2 fish

34. The blind leaders of the blind (Matthew 15:14, Luke 6:39) the Pharisees

35. "This people honors me with their lips, but their hearts ... (Matthew 15:8, Mark 7:6-7)

... are far from me."

36. Jesus gave him the name "rock." (Matthew 16:18) Peter

37. These two appeared with Jesus at the Transfiguration. (Matthew 17:1-8, Mark 9:2-8, Luke 9:28-36)

Moses and Elijah

38. These three witnessed the Transfiguration. (see references above) Peter, James, and John

39. He fulfilled the sign of Elijah. (Matthew 11:13-15) John the Baptist

40. "Foxes have holes and birds of the air have nests, but the Son of Man has ... (Matthew 8:20, Luke 9:58)

... nowhere to lay his head."

41. "No man, having put his hand to the plough, who looks back, ... (Luke 9:62)

... is fit for the kingdom of God."

42. They went to announce that the kingdom of God is near. (Luke 10:1-16)

the Seventy Disciples

43. The Messianic title that Jesus used of Himself (Matthew 26:64, Mark 14:62, Luke 22:69)

Son of Man

44. These descendants of Israel were the enemies of the Jews. (John 4:9) Samaritans

45. He could not give up his wealth and follow Jesus. (Matthew 19:16-30, Mark 10:17-31, Luke 18:18-30)

the rich, young ruler

46. "It is easier for a camel to go through the eye of a needle than ... (Matthew 19:23-24, Mark 10:24-25, Luke 18:24-25) ... for a rich man to enter the kingdom of God."

47. The shepherd left the ninety-nine to find what? (Matthew 18:12-14, Luke 15:3-7) one lost sheep

48. The woman swept her house clean to find what? (Luke 15:8-10) lost coin

49. The father met him in the road on his return. (Luke 15:11-32) Prodigal Son

50. He climbed a sycamore tree just to see Jesus. (Luke 19:1-10) Zaccheus

51. She kept the house. (Luke 10:38-42) Martha

52. She sat at Jesus' feet. (see reference above) Mary

53. He came forth from the tomb. (John 11:1-44) Lazarus

54. The high priest who unknowingly prophesied about Jesus' death (John 11:50)

Caiaphas

55. She gave out of her poverty to the treasury. (Mark 12:41-44, Luke 21:1-4) the poor widow

56. Only He knows the day and the hour of Christ's return to earth. (Matthew 24:34-36, Mark 13:30-32, Luke 21:32-33) the Father

57. He betrayed Jesus to the chief priests. (Matthew 26:14-16, Mark 14:10-11, Luke 22:3-6)

Judas Iscariot

58. The Jewish holiday when Christ had His last earthly meal (Matthew 26:17-29, Mark 14:12-25, Luke 22:7-20)

Passover

59. Where Jesus and the disciples had the Last Supper (see references above) The Upper Room

60. "This is my body" corresponds to the (see references above) bread

61. "This is the new testament in my blood" corresponds to the (Matthew 26:17-29, Mark 14:12-25, Luke 22:7-20)

wine

62. "The poor you always have with you, but ... (Matthew 26:11, Mark 14:7)

... me you do not have always."

63. The new commandment that Jesus gave His disciples (John 13:34) Love one another.

64. He said that he would never desert Jesus. (Luke 22:31-34) Peter

65. The site of Jesus' agony and suffering (Matthew 26:36, Mark 14:32) Garden of Gethsemane

66. "The spirit is willing, but ... (Matthew 26:41) ... the flesh is weak."

67. He betrayed the Lord with a kiss. (Matthew 26:47-50, Mark 14:43-45, Luke 22:47-48) Judas

68. "For all who draw the sword shall ... (Matthew 26:52) ... die by the sword."

69. She had a dream about Jesus before His trial. (Matthew 27:19) Pilate's wife

70. He was a robber and murderer released by the crowd. (Matthew 27:16-23, Mark 15:6-15, Luke 23:18-25)

Barabbas

71. He washed his hands of the decision. (Matthew 27:24) Pontius Pilate

72. He helped to carry Jesus' cross. (Matthew 27:32, Mark 15:21, Luke 23:26) Simon the Cyrene

73. The path of Jesus' suffering Via Dolorosa

74. He said, "Remember me when you come into your kingdom." (Luke 23:39-43)

Thief on the cross

75. He said, "Truly this man was the Son of God." (Matthew 27:54, Mark 15:39, Luke 23:47)

Centurion

76. He requested the body of Jesus from Pilate. (Matthew 27:57-60, Mark 15:42-46, Luke 23:50-53)

Joseph of Arimathea

77. She found the Lord's empty tomb. (Matthew 28:1-10, Mark 16:1-8, Luke 24:1-11) Mary Magdalene

78. He needed to see the nail prints for himself. (John 20:24-29) Thomas

ACTS - Scripture Verses

Acts 2:1-4
And when the day of Pentecost was fully come, they were all with one accord in one place. And suddenly there came a sound from heaven as of a rushing mighty wind, and it filled all the house where they were sitting. There appeared unto them cloven tongues like fire, and it sat upon each of them. And they were all filled with the Holy Ghost, and began to speak with other tongues.

Acts 9:3-5
And as he journeyed, he came near Damascus: and suddenly there shone round about him a light from heaven: And he fell to the earth, and heard a voice saying unto him, Saul, Saul, why persecutest thou me? And he said, Who art thou, Lord? And the Lord said, I am Jesus whom thou persecutest.

Acts 17:22-23
Then Paul stood in the midst of Mars Hill, and said, Ye men of Athens, I perceive that in all things you are very religious. For as I passed by, and beheld your devotions, I found an altar with this inscription, TO THE UNKNOWN GOD. Whom therefore ye ignorantly worship, him I declare unto you.

Acts 20:35 *It is more blessed to give than to receive.*

PAULINE EPISTLES - Scripture Verses

Galatians 3:26, 28
For you are all the children of God by faith in Christ Jesus. There is neither Jew nor Greek, there is neither bond nor free, there is neither male nor female, for you are all one in Christ Jesus.

I Corinthians 3:17 *The temple of God is holy, which temple ye are.*

I Corinthians 13:4-8
Love suffereth long, and is kind; love envieth not; love vaunteth not itself, is not puffed up, doth not behave itself unseemly, seeketh not her own, is not easily provoked, thinketh no evil; rejoiceth not in iniquity, but rejoiceth in truth; beareth all things, believeth all things, hopeth all things, endureth all things. Love never faileth.

II Timothy 4:6-8
For I am now ready to be offered, and the time of my departure is at hand. I have fought a good fight, I have finished my course, I have kept the faith. Henceforth there is laid up for me a crown of righteousness, which the Lord, the righteous judge, shall give me at that day; and not to me only but unto all them also that love his appearing.

Revelation 3:20 *Behold, I stand at the door and knock.*

Revelation 21:1-4
And I saw a new heaven and a new earth
for the first heaven and the first earth were passed away; and there was no more sea.
And I John saw the holy city, the new Jerusalem,
coming down from God out of heaven,
prepared as a bride adorned for her husband.
And I heard a great voice out of heaven saying,
Behold, the tabernacle of God is with men,
and he will dwell with them, and they shall be his people,
and God himself shall be with them, and be their God.
And God shall wipe away all tears from their eyes;
and there shall be no more death, neither sorrow,
nor crying, neither shall there be any more pain:
for the former things are passed away.

Revelation 22:13 *I am the Alpha and the Omega, the beginning and the end, the first and the last.*

ACTS & REVELATION - Drill Questions

1. Where did Jesus send His disciples? (Acts 1:7-8)
   Jerusalem, Judea, Samaria, and the world.
2. How long did Jesus remain on earth after He arose? (Acts 1:3) 40 days
3. What kind of baptism did the Apostles receive? (Acts 2:1-13) a baptism of the Spirit
4. He was chosen to replace Judas Iscariot. (Acts 1:12-26) Matthias
5. He preached to the people at Pentecost. (Acts 2:14-41) Peter
6. He prayed for his persecutors. (Acts 7:55-60) Stephen
7. "Saul, Saul, why do you ... (Acts 9:4) ... persecute me?"
8. He was sent to Saul to give him back his sight. (Acts 9:10-19) Ananias
9. The birthplace of Paul (Acts 9:11) Tarsus
10. "I shall show him how greatly he must suffer for my name's sake." (Acts 9:16)
    Paul
11. He was a god-fearing Gentile converted by Peter. (Acts 10:24-48) Cornelius
12. He was killed by Herod to discourage the Church. (Acts 12:1-2) James, brother of John
13. He was set apart with Paul to preach to the Gentiles. (Acts 13:1-3) Barnabas
14. Where did Paul preach first? (Acts 9:19-20) synagogues
15. Lystra saw them as Jupiter and Mercury. (Acts 14:8-18) Paul and Barnabas
16. It was written to correct error over the Law. Galatians
17. A meeting about Jews and Gentiles in the Church (Acts 15) Jerusalem Council
18. He accompanied Paul on his second mission. (Acts 15:36-40) Silas
19. He asked Paul for help in a dream. (Acts 16:9-10) Macedonian man
20. Where Paul addressed the men of Athens (Acts 17:22-34) Mars Hill, Areopagus
21. The most widespread Greek philosophy in Paul's time (Acts 17:18) Stoicism
22. He was an influential convert in Corinth. (Acts 18:8) Crispus
23. The largest of Paul's epistles I and II Corinthians
24. A stumbling block to Jews, foolishness to Greeks (I Corinthians 1:23)
    the message of the Cross

25. She is one body in Christ, though she has many members. (I Corinthians 12:12-13)

the Church

26. The home of Diana's Temple (Acts 19:23-41) Ephesus

27. The silversmith that started a riot in Ephesus (see reference above) Demetrius

28. The most theological of Paul's epistles Romans

29. He almost believed Paul's message. (Acts 26:1-32) King Agrippa

30. "If there be any virtue and if there be any praise, think about these." Philippians

31. "Set your affection on things above, not on things on earth." Colossians

32. He walks about like a roaring lion seeking whom he may devour. (I Peter 5:8)

Satan

33. He saw a vision of the new heaven and new earth. (Revelation 1:1-2) John

CHRISTIAN STUDIES IV

TESTS

*reproducible for classroom use

CHRISTIAN STUDIES TEST 1

(INTRODUCTION - DEUTERONOMY)

Name: ______________________ Date: ______________ Score: _________ /50

Matching: Choose the answer that best fits the description. (1 pt. each)

1. ___ where God confused the language of man
2. ___ number of days God took to create the world
3. ___ first High Priest of Israel
4. ___ the date of the Exodus
5. ___ name given to Jacob
6. ___ succeeded Moses as leader of Israel
7. ___ number of books in the New Testament
8. ___ first human beings
9. ___ where God gives Moses the Ten Commandments
10. ___ date of the call of Abraham
11. ___ man whom God used to preserve Israel during the famine in Egypt
12. ___ Greek translation of the Hebrew scriptures
13. ___ number of books in the Old Testament
14. ___ God spoke to him through his donkey
15. ___ what God appeared in to call to Moses
16. ___ man whom God used to preserve mankind during the flood
17. ___ the event in which sin entered the world
18. ___ land promised to Abraham and his descendents
19. ___ the Jewish name for the Old Testament
20. ___ punishment sent by God against the Egyptians
21. ___ offered as a sacrifice by his father
22. ___ doctrine that the Bible was completely guided and directed by God
23. ___ number of years the Israelites wandered the wilderness
24. ___ author of Pentateuch
25. ___ cities destroyed by God

A. Noah
B. 6
C. 27
D. 49/39/46
E. 40
F. Balaam
G. Tanak
H. Sodom and Gomorrah
I. Tower of Babel
J. Canaan
K. inspiration
L. Joseph
M. Isaac
N. Moses
O. Aaron
P. Mt. Sinai
Q. Israel
R. Joshua
S. 10 plagues
T. Septuagint
U. Adam and Eve
V. the Fall
W. burning bush
X. 1400 B.C.
Y. 2000 B.C.

Vocabulary: Choose the answer that best fits the definition. (1 pt. each)

1. ___ true to accomplish what has been promised
2. ___ satisfaction for wrongdoing
3. ___ tent, center of worship for the Hebrews
4. ___ a binding agreement or treaty between two parties
5. ___ separate from evil; set apart
6. ___ creation out of nothing
7. ___ image of God
8. ___ rescue, deliverance
9. ___ head of a tribe or family
10. ___ set apart for God's use

A. holy
B. redemption
C. faithful
D. covenant
E. imago Dei
F. patriarch
G. tabernacle
H. creatio ex nihilo
I. atonement
J. consecrate

List: Write out the Ten Commandments in the correct order. (Either tradition is acceptable) (10 pts.)

1. ______________________________
2. ______________________________
3. ______________________________
4. ______________________________
5. ______________________________
6. ______________________________
7. ______________________________
8. ______________________________
9. ______________________________
10. ______________________________

Scripture: Write the verse from memory. Be accurate. (5 pts.)

Exodus 3:13-14 ______________________________

____

____

____

____

Extra Credit: What is the Shema? *hint: Deut. 6:4 (3 pts.)

____

CHRISTIAN STUDIES TEST 2

(JOSHUA - ESTHER)

Name: ______________________________ Date:______________ Score: ________ /50

Matching: Choose the answer that best fits the description (1 pt. each)

1.	___ prophet taken in a chariot of fire	**A.**	Samuel
2.	___ delivered Israel from the Canaanites	**B.**	Bathsheba
3.	___ delivered Israel from the Midianites	**C.**	Rahab
4.	___ delivered Israel from the Philistines	**D.**	Deborah
5.	___ place where David built his capital city	**E.**	Rehoboam
6.	___ date the Northern Kingdom fell to Assyria	**F.**	Ruth
7.	___ wife David took from Uriah	**G.**	Jerusalem
8.	___ scribe and priest who led the second group of exiles and restored the Law	**H.**	Boaz
9.	___ prostitute who hid Israelite spies	**I.**	Saul
10.	___ city Israel defeated after crossing the Jordan River	**J.**	David
11.	___ date Israel divided into the Northern and Southern Kingdoms	**K.**	Jonathan
12.	___ son of David; built temple and palace	**L.**	Mordecai
13.	___ kinsman redeemer who marries Ruth	**M.**	Absalom
14.	___ Hebrew girl who was chosen as queen of Persia	**N.**	Solomon
15.	___ name of the Southern Kingdom	**O.**	Jereboam I
16.	___ prophet of God and final judge of Israel	**P.**	Gideon
17.	___ date the exiles first return to Jerusalem	**Q.**	Elijah
18.	___ prophet who took the place of Elijah	**R.**	Ezra
19.	___ slayer of Goliath; second king of Israel	**S.**	Samson
20.	___ devised a plot to kill all the Jews	**T.**	Nehemiah
21.	___ date the Southern Kingdom fell to Babylon	**U.**	Esther
22.	___ royal cupbearer; led third group of exiles	**V.**	Haman
23.	___ son of David who tries to take his throne	**W.**	Jericho
24.	___ first king of Northern Kingdom	**X.**	Elisha
25.	___ first king of Southern Kingdom	**Y.**	Israel
26.	___ Jew who helped Esther save the Jews	**Z.**	Judah
		AA.	931 B.C.
		AB.	722 B.C.
		AC.	586 B.C.
		AD.	536 B.C.

27. ___ name of the Northern Kingdom

28. ___ son of Saul who protects David from his father

29. ___ daughter-in-law of Naomi who chooses to stay with her

30. ___ first king of Israel

Vocabulary: Choose the answer that best fits the definition (1 pt. each)

1. ___ deliverer of Israel primarily through military means
2. ___ the foreseeing care and guidance of God in the affairs of man
3. ___ forced removal from one's native land
4. ___ supremacy of authority or rule
5. ___ conforming to the requirements set forth by God
6. ___ permanent structure, center of Hebrew worship
7. ___ state or nation ruled by a monarch or king
8. ___ a relative who preserves the family and land of a widowed woman
9. ___ government in Israel during the time of the judges when God was king
10. ___ total departure from God's commandments

A. obedience
B. kinsman redeemer
C. monarchy
D. temple
E. sovereignty
F. exile
G. providence
H. judge
I. apostasy
J. theocracy

Scripture: Write the verse from memory. Be accurate. (5 pts.)

Ruth 1:16 ____

____

____

Diagram: Complete the diagram for the Circular Nature of Judges. (5 pts.)

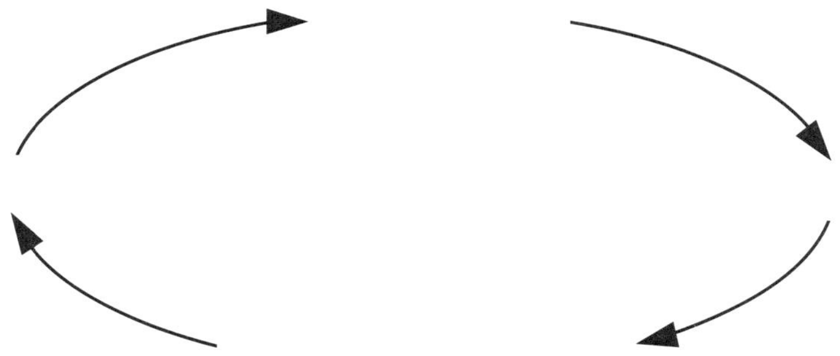

Extra Credit: (4 pts.)

1. How many judges were there in total in Israel? ______________________

2. How old was Josiah, king of Judah, when he became king? ______________________

CHRISTIAN STUDIES TEST 3

(THE PROPHETS)

Name: ________________________________ Date:______________ Score: _________ /50

Matching: Choose the answer that best fits the description (1 pt. each)

1. ___ king who threw Daniel in the lion's den
2. ___ encouraged the people to persevere in rebuilding the temple
3. ___ the primary message of the prophets
4. ___ first prophet to describe the coming final judgment of all nations
5. ___ prophet whose life reflected God's relationship with Israel
6. ___ men called by God to speak for God and guide his people
7. ___ prophet whose book was an indictment of Israel
8. ___ number of days Jonah was in the belly of the fish
9. ___ spoke of a coming Shepherd who would restore God's people
10. ___ book written by Jeremiah mourning the destruction of the temple
11. ___ king who built a golden statue of himself
12. ___ foretold the destruction of Edom for raiding Jerusalem
13. ___ section of Bible containing prophets with shorter books
14. ___ first prophet sent to Nineveh; swallowed by a fish
15. ___ given a vision of the final judgment
16. ___ first prophet to foretell the fall of the Northern and Southern Kingdoms
17. ___ unfaithful wife of Hosea
18. ___ prophet who witnessed the fall of Jerusalem
19. ___ prophet who described the coming Day of the Lord and called Judah to repent
20. ___ section of Bible containing prophets with longer books
21. ___ revealed God's plan to restore Israel and bless the world through the Messiah
22. ___ prophet whose book was a dialogue between himself and God
23. ___ second prophet sent to Nineveh
24. ___ demonstrated that Judah deserved the judgment they received
25. ___ challenged the people to remember the Law of Moses

A. Isaiah
B. Jeremiah
C. Lamentations
D. Ezekiel
E. Daniel
F. Hosea
G. Joel
H. Amos
I. Obadiah
J. Jonah
K. Micah
L. Nahum
M. Habakkuk
N. Zephaniah
O. Haggai
P. Zechariah
Q. Malachi
R. Darius
S. Nebuchadnezzar
T. Gomer
U. prophets
V. Major Prophets
W. Minor Prophets
X. repent
Y. 3

Vocabulary: Choose the answer that best fits the definition (1 pt. each)

1. ___ an accusation of guilt
2. ___ conformity to moral rightness
3. ___ a person who protects and guides a person or group
4. ___ feeling remorse and changing one's behavior
5. ___ faithfulness to obligations and commitments
6. ___ sympathy for the misfortune of others; desire to help
7. ___ a vivid picture of reality that can't be seen without God's help
8. ___ failing to act in accordance with the Law
9. ___ deserving blame for wrongdoing
10. ___ a small surviving group of people
11. ___ an expression of grief or sorrow
12. ___ the final day of judgment
13. ___ continuing in a course of action in spite of difficulties
14. ___ conversation between one or more persons
15. ___ the promised deliverer of Israel

A. dialogue
B. lament
C. repent
D. culpable
E. indictment
F. perseverance
G. unfaithful
H. Day of the Lord
I. justice
J. remnant
K. vision
L. compassion
M. fidelity
N. Messiah
O. shepherd

Scripture: Write each verse from memory. Be accurate. (5 pts. each)

Zechariah 7:9-10 ____

____

____

____

Isaiah 9:2,6 ____

____

____

____

Extra Credit: (4 pts.)

Write out Amos 5:24 from memory. ____

____

____

CHRISTIAN STUDIES TEST 4

(OLD TESTAMENT REVIEW)

Name: ______________________________ Date:______________ Score: ________ /90

Matching: Choose the answer that best fits the description. (1 pt. each)

1. ___ land promised to Abraham and his descendents
2. ___ Hebrew girl who was chosen as queen of Persia
3. ___ the beginning of knowledge
4. ___ the primary message of the prophets
5. ___ name of the Northern Kingdom
6. ___ name of the Southern Kingdom
7. ___ type of song that reflects wisdom literature
8. ___ author of Pentateuch
9. ___ place where David built his capital city
10. ___ man who, while suffering, realized comfort comes from trusting God
11. ___ type of song that expresses trust in God
12. ___ author of the majority of Proverbs
13. ___ sent to Nineveh; swallowed by a fish
14. ___ foretold the coming of the Messiah
15. ___ type of song that praises God for who he is
16. ___ wrote Lamentations when Jerusalem was destroyed
17. ___ two aspects of poetry
18. ___ first king of Israel
19. ___ offered as a sacrifice by his father
20. ___ type of song that expresses sadness or fear
21. ___ first High Priest of Israel
22. ___ prostitute who hid Israelite spies
23. ___ type of song focused on the Davidic Monarchy
24. ___ prophet taken in a chariot of fire
25. ___ aspect of Hebrew poetry that rhymes ideas
26. ___ first human beings

A. Aaron
B. Adam and Eve
C. Canaan
D. confidence
E. David
F. Elijah
G. Esther
H. fear of God
I. Isaac
J. Isaiah
K. Israel
L. Jeremiah
M. Jerusalem
N. Job
O. Jonah
P. Judah
Q. kingship
R. lament
S. Moses
T. Noah
U. parallelism
V. praise
W. Rahab
X. repent
Y. rhythm and rhyme
Z. Samuel
AA. Saul
AB. Solomon
AC. thanksgiving
AD. wisdom

27. ___ author of the majority of the Psalms

28. ___ type of song that thanks God for answering prayers

29. ___ prophet of God and final judge of Israel

30. ___ man whom God used to preserve mankind during the flood

Matching: Choose the answer that best fits the description. (1 pt. each)

1. ___ Jewish name for the Old Testmant
2. ___ king who built a golden statue of himself
3. ___ wife David took from Uriah
4. ___ date Israel divided into the Northern and Southern Kingdoms
5. ___ number of books in the Old Testament
6. ___ date the Northern Kingdom fell to Assyria
7. ___ date of the Exodus
8. ___ slayer of Goliath; second king of Israel
9. ___ Greek translation of the Hebrew scriptures
10. ___ name given to Jacob
11. ___ date the exiles first return to Jerusalem
12. ___ son of David; built temple and palace
13. ___ man used by God to preserve Israel during the famine in Egypt
14. ___ where God gives Moses the Ten Commandments
15. ___ number of books in the New Testament
16. ___ section of Bible containing prophets with longer books
17. ___ section of Bible containing prophets with shorter books
18. ___ date Southern Kingdom fell to Babylon
19. ___ succeeded Moses as leader of Israel
20. ___ date of the Call of Abraham

A. 27
B. 49/39/46
C. 536 B.C.
D. 586 B.C.
E. 722 B.C.
F. 931 B.C.
G. 1400 B.C.
H. 2000 B.C.
I. Bathsheba
J. David
K. Israel
L. Joseph
M. Joshua
N. Major Prophets
O. Minor Prophets
P. Mt. Sinai
Q. Nebuchadnezzar
R. Septuagint
S. Solomon
T. Tanak

Scripture: Write each verse from memory. Be accurate. (5 pts. each)

Exodus 3:13-14 ____

____

____

____

____

Proverbs 15:1-2 ____

____

____

Vocabulary: Choose the answer that best fits the definition. (1 pt. each)

1. ___ a category of artistic work
2. ___ set apart for God's use
3. ___ a figure of speech that compares two unlike things using "like" or "as"
4. ___ tent, center of worship for the Hebrews
5. ___ permanent structure, center of worship for the Hebrews
6. ___ something worthless or pointless
7. ___ a feeling of relief from affliction
8. ___ a vivid picture of reality that can't be seen without God's help
9. ___ the promised deliverer of Judah
10. ___ government in Israel during the time of the judges when God was king
11. ___ feeling remorse and changing one's behavior
12. ___ creation out of nothing
13. ___ satisfaction for wrongdoing
14. ___ a binding agreement or treaty between two parties
15. ___ song of praise to God
16. ___ sympathy for the misfortune of others; desire to help
17. ___ all the people of God gathering in worship
18. ___ total departure from God's commandments
19. ___ a figure of speech that compares two unlike things without using "like" or "as"
20. ___ deliverer of Israel primarily through military means
21. ___ the final day of judgment
22. ___ forced removal from one's native land
23. ___ a relative who preserves the family and land of a widowed woman
24. ___ a small surviving group of people
25. ___ the skill of living in a godly way

A. apostasy
B. atonement
C. comfort
D. compassion
E. consecrate
F. corporate worship
G. covenant
H. creatio ex nihilo
I. Day of the Lord
J. exile
K. genre
L. judge
M. kinsman redeemer
N. Messiah
O. metaphor
P. psalm
Q. remnant
R. repent
S. simile
T. tabernacle
U. temple
V. theocracy
W. vanity
X. vision
Y. wisdom

Matching: Draw a line from the type of Hebrew Parallelism to its description. (5 pts.)

Synonymous/ Repeating	The first part makes a statement and the second part completes the idea.
Antithetic/ Opposite	The first part makes a statement and the second part repeats the statement in a different way.
Synthetic/ Completing	The first part makes a statement and the second part tells the opposite of that statement.

Extra Credit: (8 pts.)

Write out Psalm 1 from memory. Be accurate.

CHRISTIAN STUDIES TEST 5

(INTERTESTAMENTAL PERIOD - ACTS)

Name: ______________________________ Date:______________ Score: ________ /50

Matching: Choose the answer that best fits the description. (1 pt. each)

1. ___ first Christian martyr
2. ___ rule of the Maccabean family
3. ___ town in which Jesus was born
4. ___ date Pompey conquered Palestine
5. ___ "disciple whom Jesus loved"
6. ___ recipient of Luke's two-volume work
7. ___ religious leaders focused on maintaining the purity of the Law
8. ___ "make disciples of all nations"
9. ___ date of the birth of Christ
10. ___ Jesus' first miracle
11. ___ Pharisee who was confronted by Jesus and made an apostle
12. ___ given by Jesus at Pentecost
13. ___ date of the Maccabean Revolt
14. ___ tax collector who became a disciple
15. ___ recaptured the temple from the Seleucids
16. ___ Jewish celebration commemorating the recapturing of the temple
17. ___ Gospels that have similar content and style
18. ___ attendant and writer for Peter
19. ___ parents of Jesus
20. ___ elderly priest who led a revolt against Syria
21. ___ physician and historian
22. ___ witness in Samaria
23. ___ Jewish group that resisted Hellenization; "pious ones"
24. ___ disciple who preached at Pentecost

A. turning water into wine
B. Theophilus
C. Synoptic Gospels
D. Stephen
E. Pompey
F. Philip
G. Pharisees
H. Peter
I. Pax Romana
J. Paul
K. Mark
L. Matthew
M. Mattathias
N. Luke
O. Judas Maccabeus
P. Joseph and Mary
Q. John the Baptist
R. John
S. Holy Spirit
T. Herod
U. Hasmonean Dynasty
V. Hasidim
W. Hanukkah
X. Great Commission
Y. Bethlehem
Z. 167-142 B.C.
AA. 63 B.C.
AB. 4 B.C.

25. ___ conquered Palestine for Rome

26. ___ Roman governor of Judea at the time of Jesus' birth

27. ___ Peace of Rome

28. ___ man who preached repentance and baptized in the Jordan River

Vocabulary: Choose the answer that best fits the definition. (1 pt. each)

1. ___ Jesus' method of teaching by using stories
2. ___ chosen Messiah
3. ___ local place of worship for Jews during the diaspora
4. ___ a person who is not Jewish
5. ___ an official messenger of the gospel
6. ___ the Roman name for Canaan
7. ___ the good news of the salvation provided by Jesus' life, death, and resurrection
8. ___ deliverance from the power and penalty of sin
9. ___ the spreading of the Greek culture and way of life
10. ___ a person who testifies to events or facts within his own knowledge
11. ___ spread of Jews all over the Roman Empire
12. ___ one who chooses to suffer death rather than renounce religious beliefs

A. apostle
B. gospel
C. Palestine
D. Gentile
E. martyr
F. synagogue
G. diaspora
H. salvation
I. Christ
J. Hellenization
K. parable
L. witness

Scripture: Write the verse from memory. Be accurate. (5 pts.)

Mark 8:34-37 ____

____

____

____

____

Short Answer: Write the answer that best completes the sentence. (1 pt. each)

1. An important theme present throughout the New Testament is ____.

2. The disciples became witnesses to ____.

Extra Credit: Write out Acts 1:8 from memory. (4 pts.)

CHRISTIAN STUDIES TEST 6

(INTERTESTAMENTAL PERIOD AND NEW TESTAMENT REVIEW)

Name: ______________________________ Date:______________ Score: ________ /100

Matching: Choose the answer that best fits the description. (1 pt. each)

1. ___ ultimate example of humility
2. ___ Jewish celebration commemorating the recapturing of the temple
3. ___ Jesus' first miracle
4. ___ Emperor of Rome who actively persecuted Christians
5. ___ Pharisee confronted by Jesus and made an apostle
6. ___ Peace of Rome
7. ___ according to Paul the gospel makes all men ...
8. ___ date of the Maccabean Revolt
9. ___ disciple who preached at Pentecost
10. ___ first Christian martyr
11. ___ physician and historian
12. ___ letters written by Paul
13. ___ rule of the Maccabean family
14. ___ date of the birth of Christ
15. ___ attendant and writer for Peter
16. ___ man who preached repentance and baptized in the Jordan River
17. ___ wrote Revelation while exiled on the island of Patmos
18. ___ conquered Palestine for Rome
19. ___ witness in Samaria
20. ___ letters written to a general audience
21. ___ religious leaders focused on maintaining the purity of the Law
22. ___ parents of Jesus
23. ___ date Pompey conquered Palestine
24. ___ "make disciples of all nations"
25. ___ according to Paul, man is justified by ...

A. 4 B.C.
B. 63 B.C.
C. 167-142 B.C.
D. Bethlehem
E. equal
F. faith
G. General Epistles
H. Great Commission
I. Hanukkah
J. Hasidim
K. Hasmonean Dynasty
L. Herod
M. Holy Spirit
N. James
O. Jesus
P. John
Q. John the Baptist
R. Joseph and Mary
S. Judas Maccabeus
T. Luke
U. Mattathias
V. Matthew
W. Mark
X. Nero
Y. Pastoral Letters
Z. Paul
AA. Pauline Epistles
AB. Pax Romana
AC. Peter
AD. Pharisees
AE. Philip

26. ___ leader in the church in Jerusalem
27. ___ town in which Jesus was born
28. ___ Roman governor of Judea at the time of Jesus' birth
29. ___ tax collector who became a disciple
30. ___ recipient of Luke's two-volume work
31. ___ letters of instruction and guidance for leaders
32. ___ Jewish group that resisted Hellenization; "pious ones"
33. ___ elderly priest who led revolt against Syria
34. ___ given by Jesus when he ascended
35. ___ letters written while Paul was under house arrest
36. ___ recaptured the temple from the Seleucids
37. ___ Gospels that have similar content and style

AF. Pompey
AG. Prison Letters
AH. Stephen
AI. Synoptic Gospels
AJ. Theophilus
AK. turning water to wine

List: Complete each list. (1 pt. each)

The 3 types of addressees for the epistles:

1. ______________________
2. ______________________
3. ______________________

The Prison Letters:

1. ______________________
2. ______________________
3. ______________________
4. ______________________

The three sections of an epistle:

1. ______________________
2. ______________________
3. ______________________

The Pastoral Letters:

1. ______________________
2. ______________________
3. ______________________

Books Containing Apocalyptic Literature:

1. ______________________
2. ______________________
3. ______________________

Short Answer: Write the answer that best completes the sentence. (1 pt.)

The disciples became witnesses to ____

____

Vocabulary: Choose the answer that best fits the definition. (1 pt. each)

1. ____ a sacrifice that bears God's wrath
2. ____ a person who is not Jewish
3. ____ study of God
4. ____ the study of the last things
5. ____ chosen Messiah
6. ____ the spreading of the Greek culture and way of life
7. ____ trust in God and his promises
8. ____ a person who testifies to events or facts within his own knowledge
9. ____ made right with God
10. ____ readiness and willingness to give
11. ____ the Roman name for Canaan
12. ____ persistence in spite of difficulties
13. ____ false teaching
14. ____ Jesus' method of teaching using stories
15. ____ one who chooses to suffer death rather than renounce his religious beliefs
16. ____ inward hope despite circumstances
17. ____ separation because of different opinions
18. ____ a revelation of hidden realities given by God
19. ____ deliverance from the power and penalty of sin
20. ____ to make a friend of an enemy
21. ____ torturing or killing people because of their beliefs
22. ____ spread of Jews all over the Roman Empire
23. ____ an official messenger of the gospel
24. ____ ancient belief that considered all matter to be evil and only the spiritual to be good
25. ____ language that uses images instead of direct expression
26. ____ God's anger and judgment towards sin
27. ____ local place of worship for Jews during the diaspora
28. ____ ground for belief or disbelief; proof
29. ____ unearned favor and love of God
30. ____ the good news of the salvation provided by Jesus' life, death, and resurrection
31. ____ considering others more important than yourself

A. apocalypse
B. apostle
C. Christ
D. diaspora
E. division
F. eschatology
G. evidence
H. faith
I. generosity
J. Gentile
K. gospel
L. Gnosticism
M. grace
N. Hellenization
O. heresy
P. humility
Q. joy
R. justification
S. martyr
T. Palestine
U. parable
V. persecution
W. perseverance
X. propitiation
Y. reconciliation
Z. salvation
AA. symbolism
AB. synagogue
AC. theology
AD. witness
AE. wrath

Scripture: Write each verse from memory. Be accurate. (5 pts. each)

I Corinthians 13:4-8 ____

Ephesians 2:8-9 ____

II Timothy 3:16-17 ____

Extra Credit: Write each verse from memory (4 pts. each)

Mark 8:34-37 ____

Revelation 21:3-4 ____

CHRISTIAN STUDIES TEST 1

(INTRODUCTION - DEUTERONOMY)

Name: ______________________________ Date:______________ Score: ________ /50

Matching: Choose the answer that best fits the description. (1 pt. each)

1. __I__ where God confused the language of man
2. __B__ number of days God took to create the world
3. __O__ first High Priest of Israel
4. __X__ the date of the Exodus
5. __Q__ name given to Jacob
6. __R__ succeeded Moses as leader of Israel
7. __C__ number of books in the New Testament
8. __U__ first human beings
9. __P__ where God gives Moses the Ten Commandments
10. __Y__ date of the call of Abraham
11. __L__ man whom God used to preserve Israel during the famine in Egypt
12. __T__ Greek translation of the Hebrew scriptures
13. __D__ number of books in the Old Testament
14. __F__ God spoke to him through his donkey
15. __W__ what God appeared in to call to Moses
16. __A__ man whom God used to preserve mankind during the flood
17. __V__ the event in which sin entered the world
18. __J__ land promised to Abraham and his descendents
19. __G__ the Jewish name for the Old Testament
20. __S__ punishment sent by God against the Egyptians
21. __M__ offered as a sacrifice by his father
22. __K__ doctrine that the Bible was completely guided and directed by God
23. __E__ number of years the Israelites wandered the wilderness
24. __N__ author of Pentateuch
25. __H__ cities destroyed by God

A. Noah
B. 6
C. 27
D. 49/39/46
E. 40
F. Balaam
G. Tanak
H. Sodom and Gomorrah
I. Tower of Babel
J. Canaan
K. inspiration
L. Joseph
M. Isaac
N. Moses
O. Aaron
P. Mt. Sinai
Q. Israel
R. Joshua
S. 10 plagues
T. Septuagint
U. Adam and Eve
V. the Fall
W. burning bush
X. 1400 B.C.
Y. 2000 B.C.

Vocabulary: Choose the answer that best fits the definition. (1 pt. each)

1. C true to accomplish what has been promised
2. I satisfaction for wrongdoing
3. G tent, center of worship for the Hebrews
4. D a binding agreement or treaty between two parties
5. A separate from evil; set apart
6. H creation out of nothing
7. E image of God
8. B rescue, deliverance
9. F head of a tribe or family
10. J set apart for God's use

A. holy
B. redemption
C. faithful
D. covenant
E. imago Dei
F. patriarch
G. tabernacle
H. creatio ex nihilo
I. atonement
J. consecrate

List: Write out the Ten Commandments in the correct order. (Either tradition is acceptable) (10 pts.)

	Catholic/Lutheran	Protestant
1.	I am the Lord your God: you shall have no gods before me.	I am the Lord your God: you shall have no gods before me.
2.	You shall not take the name of the Lord your God in vain.	You shall not make any graven images.
3.	Remember the Sabbath and keep it holy.	You shall not take the name of the Lord your God in vain.
4.	Honor thy father and mother.	Remember the Sabbath and keep it holy.
5.	Thou shall not kill.	Honor thy father and mother.
6.	Thou shall not commit adultery.	You shall not kill.
7.	Thou shall not steal.	You shall not commit adultery.
8.	Thou shall not bear false witness against your neighbor.	You shall not steal.
9.	Thou shall not covet your neighbor's wife.	You shall not bear false witness against your neighbor.
10.	Thou shall not covet your neighbor's goods.	You shall not covet thy neighbor's house nor his wife nor anything that belongs to him.

Scripture: Write the verse from memory. Be accurate. (5 pts.)

Exodus 3:13-14 And Moses said unto God, Behold, when I come unto the children of Israel and shall say unto them, The God of your fathers has sent me unto you and they shall say unto me, What is his name? What shall I say unto them? And God said unto Moses, I AM THAT I AM; and he said, Thus shalt you say unto the children of Israel, I AM hath sent me unto you..

Extra Credit: What is the Shema? *hint: Deut. 6:4 (3 pts.)

"Hear, O Israel: The Lord our God, the Lord is one."

ANSWER KEY

CHRISTIAN STUDIES TEST 2

(JOSHUA - ESTHER)

Name: ______________________________ Date: ______________ Score: ________ /50

Matching: Choose the answer that best fits the description (1 pt. each)

1. __Q__ prophet taken in a chariot of fire
2. __D__ delivered Israel from the Canaanites
3. __P__ delivered Israel from the Midianites
4. __S__ delivered Israel from the Philistines
5. __G__ place where David built his capital city
6. __AB__ date the Northern Kingdom fell to Assyria
7. __B__ wife David took from Uriah
8. __R__ scribe and priest who led the second group of exiles and restored the Law
9. __C__ prostitute who hid Israelite spies
10. __W__ city Israel defeated after crossing the Jordan River
11. __AA__ date Israel divided into the Northern and Southern Kingdoms
12. __N__ son of David; built temple and palace
13. __H__ kinsman redeemer who marries Ruth
14. __U__ Hebrew girl who was chosen as queen of Persia
15. __Z__ name of the Southern Kingdom
16. __A__ prophet of God and final judge of Israel
17. __AD__ date the exiles first return to Jerusalem
18. __X__ prophet who took the place of Elijah
19. __J__ slayer of Goliath; second king of Israel
20. __V__ devised a plot to kill all the Jews
21. __AC__ date the Southern Kingdom fell to Babylon
22. __T__ royal cupbearer; led third group of exiles
23. __M__ son of David who tries to take his throne
24. __O__ first king of Northern Kingdom
25. __E__ first king of Southern Kingdom
26. __L__ Jew who helped Esther save the Jews

A. Samuel
B. Bathsheba
C. Rahab
D. Deborah
E. Rehoboam
F. Ruth
G. Jerusalem
H. Boaz
I. Saul
J. David
K. Jonathan
L. Mordecai
M. Absalom
N. Solomon
O. Jereboam I
P. Gideon
Q. Elijah
R. Ezra
S. Samson
T. Nehemiah
U. Esther
V. Haman
W. Jericho
X. Elisha
Y. Israel
Z. Judah
AA. 931 B.C.
AB. 722 B.C.
AC. 586 B.C.
AD. 536 B.C.

27. __Y__ name of the Northern Kingdom

28. __K__ son of Saul who protects David from his father

29. __F__ daughter-in-law of Naomi who chooses to stay with her

30. __I__ first king of Israel

Vocabulary: Choose the answer that best fits the definition (1 pt. each)

1. __H__ deliverer of Israel primarily through military means
2. __G__ the foreseeing care and guidance of God in the affairs of man
3. __F__ forced removal from one's native land
4. __E__ supremacy of authority or rule
5. __A__ conforming to the requirements set forth by God
6. __D__ permanent structure, center of Hebrew worship
7. __C__ state or nation ruled by a monarch or king
8. __B__ a relative who preserves the family and land of a widowed woman
9. __J__ government in Israel during the time of the judges when God was king
10. __I__ total departure from God's commandments

A. obedience
B. kinsman redeemer
C. monarchy
D. temple
E. sovereignty
F. exile
G. providence
H. judge
I. apostasy
J. theocracy

Scripture: Write the verse from memory. Be accurate. (5 pts.)

Ruth 1:16 And Ruth said, Entreat me not to leave thee, or to return from following after thee; for whither thou goest, I will go, and where thou lodgest I will lodge: thy people shall be my people, and thy God, my God.

Diagram: Complete the diagram for the Circular Nature of Judges. (5 pts.)

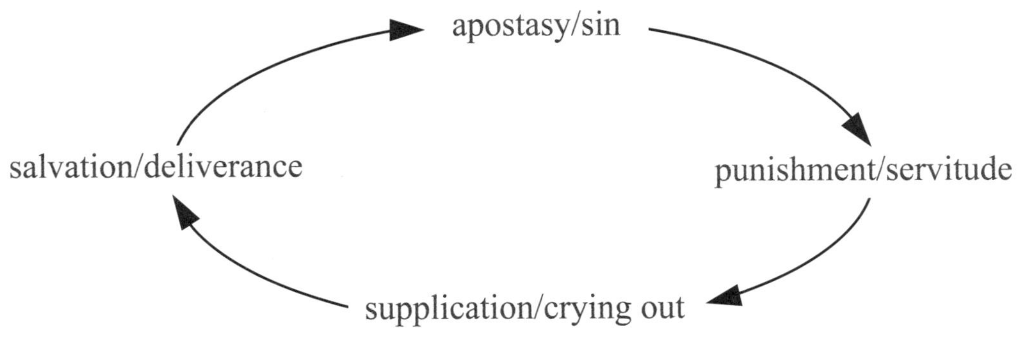

Extra Credit: (4 pts.)

1. How many judges were there in total in Israel? 12
2. How old was Josiah, king of Judah, when he became king? 8 years old

CHRISTIAN STUDIES TEST 3

(THE PROPHETS)

Name: ______________________________ Date: ______________ Score: ________ /50

Matching: Choose the answer that best fits the description (1 pt. each)

1. R king who threw Daniel in the lion's den
2. O encouraged the people to persevere in rebuilding the temple
3. X the primary message of the prophets
4. N first prophet to describe the coming final judgment of all nations
5. F prophet whose life reflected God's relationship with Israel
6. U men called by God to speak for God and guide his people
7. K prophet whose book was an indictment of Israel
8. Y number of days Jonah was in the belly of the fish
9. P spoke of a coming Shepherd who would restore God's people
10. C book written by Jeremiah mourning the destruction of the temple
11. S king who built a golden statue of himself
12. I foretold the destruction of Edom for raiding Jerusalem
13. W section of Bible containing prophets with shorter books
14. J first prophet sent to Nineveh; swallowed by a fish
15. E given a vision of the final judgment
16. H first prophet to foretell the fall of the Northern and Southern Kingdoms
17. T unfaithful wife of Hosea
18. B prophet who witnessed the fall of Jerusalem
19. G prophet who described the coming Day of the Lord and called Judah to repent
20. V section of Bible containing prophets with longer books
21. A revealed God's plan to restore Israel and bless the world
    M through the Messiah
22. L prophet whose book was a dialogue between himself and God
23. D second prophet sent to Nineveh
24. Q demonstrated that Judah deserved the judgment they received
25. ___ challenged the people to remember the Law of Moses

- **A.** Isaiah
- **B.** Jeremiah
- **C.** Lamentations
- **D.** Ezekiel
- **E.** Daniel
- **F.** Hosea
- **G.** Joel
- **H.** Amos
- **I.** Obadiah
- **J.** Jonah
- **K.** Micah
- **L.** Nahum
- **M.** Habakkuk
- **N.** Zephaniah
- **O.** Haggai
- **P.** Zechariah
- **Q.** Malachi
- **R.** Darius
- **S.** Nebuchadnezzar
- **T.** Gomer
- **U.** prophets
- **V.** Major Prophets
- **W.** Minor Prophets
- **X.** repent
- **Y.** 3

Vocabulary: Choose the answer that best fits the definition (1 pt. each)

1. E an accusation of guilt
2. I conformity to moral rightness
3. O a person who protects and guides a person or group
4. C feeling remorse and changing one's behavior
5. M faithfulness to obligations and commitments
6. L sympathy for the misfortune of others; desire to help
7. K a vivid picture of reality that can't be seen without God's help
8. G failing to act in accordance with the Law
9. D deserving blame for wrongdoing
10. J a small surviving group of people
11. B an expression of grief or sorrow
12. H the final day of judgment
13. F continuing in a course of action in spite of difficulties
14. A conversation between one or more persons
15. N the promised deliverer of Israel

A. dialogue
B. lament
C. repent
D. culpable
E. indictment
F. perseverance
G. unfaithful
H. Day of the Lord
I. justice
J. remnant
K. vision
L. compassion
M. fidelity
N. Messiah
O. shepherd

Scripture: Write each verse from memory. Be accurate. (5 pts. each)

Zechariah 7:9-10 Thus speaketh the LORD of hosts, saying, Execute true judgment, and shew mercy and compassions every man to his brother: And oppress not the widow, nor the fatherless, the stranger, nor the poor; and let none of you imagine evil against his brother in your heart.

Isaiah 9:2,6 The people that walked in darkness have seen a great light. For unto us a child is born, unto us a son is given: and the government shall be upon his shoulder; and his name shall be called Wonderful, Counsellor, The mighty God, The everlasting Father, The Prince of Peace.

Extra Credit: (4 pts.)

Write out Amos 5:24 from memory. But let judgment run down as waters, and righteousness as a mighty stream.

CHRISTIAN STUDIES TEST 4

(OLD TESTAMENT REVIEW)

Name: ______________________________ Date: ______________ Score: ________ /90

Matching: Choose the answer that best fits the description. (1 pt. each)

1. __C__ land promised to Abraham and his descendents
2. __G__ Hebrew girl who was chosen as queen of Persia
3. __H__ the beginning of knowledge
4. __X__ the primary message of the prophets
5. __K__ name of the Northern Kingdom
6. __P__ name of the Southern Kingdom
7. __AD__ type of song that reflects wisdom literature
8. __S__ author of Pentateuch
9. __M__ place where David built his capital city
10. __N__ man who, while suffering, realized comfort comes from trusting God
11. __D__ type of song that expresses trust in God
12. __AB__ author of the majority of Proverbs
13. __O__ sent to Nineveh; swallowed by a fish
14. __J__ foretold the coming of the Messiah
15. __V__ type of song that praises God for who he is
16. __L__ wrote Lamentations when Jerusalem was destroyed
17. __Y__ two aspects of poetry
18. __AA__ first king of Israel
19. __I__ offered as a sacrifice by his father
20. __R__ type of song that expresses sadness or fear
21. __A__ first High Priest of Israel
22. __W__ prostitute who hid Israelite spies
23. __Q__ type of song focused on the Davidic Monarchy
24. __F__ prophet taken in a chariot of fire
25. __U__ aspect of Hebrew poetry that rhymes ideas
26. __B__ first human beings

A. Aaron
B. Adam and Eve
C. Canaan
D. confidence
E. David
F. Elijah
G. Esther
H. fear of God
I. Isaac
J. Isaiah
K. Israel
L. Jeremiah
M. Jerusalem
N. Job
O. Jonah
P. Judah
Q. kingship
R. lament
S. Moses
T. Noah
U. parallelism
V. praise
W. Rahab
X. repent
Y. rhythm and rhyme
Z. Samuel
AA. Saul
AB. Solomon
AC. thanksgiving
AD. wisdom

27. E author of the majority of the Psalms

28. AC type of song that thanks God for answering prayers

29. Z prophet of God and final judge of Israel

30. T man whom God used to preserve mankind during the flood

Matching: Choose the answer that best fits the description. (1 pt. each)

1. T Jewish name for the Old Testment
2. Q king who built a golden statue of himself
3. I wife David took from Uriah
4. F date Israel divided into the Northern and Southern Kingdoms
5. B number of books in the Old Testament
6. E date the Northern Kingdom fell to Assyria
7. G date of the Exodus
8. J slayer of Goliath; second king of Israel
9. R Greek translation of the Hebrew scriptures
10. K name given to Jacob
11. C date the exiles first return to Jerusalem
12. S son of David; built temple and palace
13. L man used by God to preserve Israel during the famine in Egypt
14. P where God gives Moses the Ten Commandments
15. A number of books in the New Testament
16. N section of Bible containing prophets with longer books
17. O section of Bible containing prophets with shorter books
18. D date Southern Kingdom fell to Babylon
19. M succeeded Moses as leader of Israel
20. H date of the Call of Abraham

A. 27
B. 49/39/46
C. 536 B.C.
D. 586 B.C.
E. 722 B.C.
F. 931 B.C.
G. 1400 B.C.
H. 2000 B.C.
I. Bathsheba
J. David
K. Israel
L. Joseph
M. Joshua
N. Major Prophets
O. Minor Prophets
P. Mt. Sinai
Q. Nebuchadnezzar
R. Septuagint
S. Solomon
T. Tanak

Scripture: Write each verse from memory. Be accurate. (5 pts. each)

Exodus 3:13-14 And Moses said unto God, Behold, when I come unto the children of Israel, and shall say unto them, The God of your fathers hath sent me unto you; and they shall say to me, What is his name? What shall I say unto them? And God said unto Moses, I AM THAT I AM: and he said, Thus shalt you say unto the children of Israel, I AM hath sent me unto you.

Proverbs 15:1-2 A soft answer turneth away wrath: but grievous words stir up anger. The tongue of the wise useth knowledge aright : but the mouth of fools poureth out foolishness.

Vocabulary: Choose the answer that best fits the definition. (1 pt. each)

1. K a category of artistic work
2. E set apart for God's use
3. S a figure of speech that compares two unlike things using "like" or "as"
4. T tent, center of worship for the Hebrews
5. U permanent structure, center of worship for the Hebrews
6. W something worthless or pointless
7. C a feeling of relief from affliction
8. X a vivid picture of reality that can't be seen without God's help
9. N the promised deliverer of Judah
10. V government in Israel during the time of the judges when God was king
11. R feeling remorse and changing one's behavior
12. H creation out of nothing
13. B satisfaction for wrongdoing
14. G a binding agreement or treaty between two parties
15. P song of praise to God
16. D sympathy for the misfortune of others; desire to help
17. F all the people of God gathering in worship
18. A total departure from God's commandments
19. O a figure of speech that compares two unlike things without using "like" or "as"
20. L deliverer of Israel primarily through military means
21. I the final day of judgment
22. J forced removal from one's native land
23. M a relative who preserves the family and land of a widowed woman
24. Q a small surviving group of people
25. Y the skill of living in a godly way

A. apostasy
B. atonement
C. comfort
D. compassion
E. consecrate
F. corporate worship
G. covenant
H. creatio ex nihilo
I. Day of the Lord
J. exile
K. genre
L. judge
M. kinsman redeemer
N. Messiah
O. metaphor
P. psalm
Q. remnant
R. repent
S. simile
T. tabernacle
U. temple
V. theocracy
W. vanity
X. vision
Y. wisdom

Matching: Draw a line from the type of Hebrew Parallelism to its description. (5 pts.)

Synonymous/ Repeating

Antithetic/ Opposite

Synthetic/ Completing

The first part makes a statement and the second part completes the idea.

The first part makes a statement and the second part repeats the statement in a different way.

The first part makes a statement and the second part tells the opposite of that statement.

Extra Credit: (8 pts.)

Write out Psalm 1 from memory. Be accurate.

Blessed is the man that walketh not in the counsel of the ungodly, nor standeth in the way of sinners, nor sitteth in the seat of the scornful.

But his delight is in the law of the Lord; and in his law doth he meditate day and night.

And he shall be like a tree planted by the rivers of water, that bringeth forth his fruit in his season; his leaf also shall not wither; and whatsoever he doeth shall prosper.

The ungodly are not so; but are like the chaff which the wind driveth away.

Therefore the ungodly shall not stand in the judgment, nor sinners in the congregation of the righteous.

For the Lord knoweth the way of the righteous: but the way of the ungodly shall perish.

CHRISTIAN STUDIES TEST 5

(INTERTESTAMENTAL PERIOD - ACTS)

Name: ________________________________ Date:______________ Score: _________ /50

Matching: Choose the answer that best fits the description. (1 pt. each)

1. D first Christian martyr
2. U rule of the Maccabean family
3. Y town in which Jesus was born
4. AA date Pompey conquered Palestine
5. R "disciple whom Jesus loved"
6. B recipient of Luke's two-volume work
7. G religious leaders focused on maintaining the purity of the Law
8. X "make disciples of all nations"
9. AB date of the birth of Christ
10. A Jesus' first miracle
11. J Pharisee who was confronted by Jesus and made an apostle
12. S given by Jesus at Pentecost
13. Z date of the Maccabean Revolt
14. L tax collector who became a disciple
15. O recaptured the temple from the Seleucids
16. W Jewish celebration commemorating the recapturing of the temple
17. C Gospels that have similar content and style
18. K attendant and writer for Peter
19. P parents of Jesus
20. M elderly priest who led a revolt against Syria
21. N physician and historian
22. F witness in Samaria
23. V Jewish group that resisted Hellenization; "pious ones"
24. H disciple who preached at Pentecost

A. turning water into wine
B. Theophilus
C. Synoptic Gospels
D. Stephen
E. Pompey
F. Philip
G. Pharisees
H. Peter
I. Pax Romana
J. Paul
K. Mark
L. Matthew
M. Mattathias
N. Luke
O. Judas Maccabeus
P. Joseph and Mary
Q. John the Baptist
R. John
S. Holy Spirit
T. Herod
U. Hasmonean Dynasty
V. Hasidim
W. Hanukkah
X. Great Commission
Y. Bethlehem
Z. 167-142 B.C.
AA. 63 B.C.
AB. 4 B.C.

ANSWER KEY

25. E conquered Palestine for Rome

26. T Roman governor of Judea at the time of Jesus' birth

27. I Peace of Rome

28. Q man who preached repentance and baptized in the Jordan River

Vocabulary: Choose the answer that best fits the definition. (1 pt. each)

1. K Jesus' method of teaching by using stories
2. I chosen Messiah
3. F local place of worship for Jews during the diaspora
4. D a person who is not Jewish
5. A an official messenger of the gospel
6. C the Roman name for Canaan
7. B the good news of the salvation provided by Jesus' life, death, and resurrection
8. H deliverance from the power and penalty of sin
9. J the spreading of the Greek culture and way of life
10. L a person who testifies to events or facts within his own knowledge
11. G spread of Jews all over the Roman Empire
12. E one who chooses to suffer death rather than renounce religious beliefs

A. apostle
B. gospel
C. Palestine
D. Gentile
E. martyr
F. synagogue
G. diaspora
H. salvation
I. Christ
J. Hellenization
K. parable
L. witness

Scripture: Write the verse from memory. Be accurate. (5 pts.)

Mark 8:34-37 Whosoever will come after me, let him deny himself and take up his cross and follow me. For whosoever will save his life shall lose it; but whosoever shall lose his life for my sake and the gospel's, the same shall save it. For what shall it profit a man, if he shall gain the whole world, and lose his own soul? Or what shall a man give in exchange for his soul?

Short Answer: Write the answer that best completes the sentence. (1 pt. each)

1. An important theme present throughout the New Testament is already, but not yet.

2. The disciples became witnesses to Jerusalem, Judea and Samaria, and all the earth.

Extra Credit: Write out Acts 1:8 from memory. (4 pts.)

But ye shall receive power, after that the Holy Ghost is come upon you: and ye shall be witnesses unto me both in Jerusalem, and in all Judaea, and in Samaria, and unto the uttermost part of the earth.

CHRISTIAN STUDIES TEST 6

(INTERTESTAMENTAL PERIOD AND NEW TESTAMENT REVIEW)

Name: ______________________ Date: ____________ Score: ________ /100

Matching: Choose the answer that best fits the description. (1 pt. each)

1. O ultimate example of humility
2. I Jewish celebration commemorating the recapturing of the temple
3. AK Jesus' first miracle
4. X Emperor of Rome who actively persecuted Christians
5. Z Pharisee confronted by Jesus and made an apostle
6. AB Peace of Rome
7. E according to Paul the gospel makes all men ...
8. C date of the Maccabean Revolt
9. AC disciple who preached at Pentecost
10. AH first Christian martyr
11. T physician and historian
12. AA letters written by Paul
13. K rule of the Maccabean family
14. A date of the birth of Christ
15. W attendant and writer for Peter
16. Q man who preached repentance and baptized in the Jordan River
17. P wrote Revelation while exiled on the island of Patmos
18. AF conquered Palestine for Rome
19. AE witness in Samaria
20. G letters written to a general audience
21. AD religious leaders focused on maintaining the purity of the Law
22. R parents of Jesus
23. B date Pompey conquered Palestine
24. H "make disciples of all nations"
25. F according to Paul, man is justified by ...

A. 4 B.C.
B. 63 B.C.
C. 167-142 B.C.
D. Bethlehem
E. equal
F. faith
G. General Epistles
H. Great Commission
I. Hanukkah
J. Hasidim
K. Hasmonean Dynasty
L. Herod
M. Holy Spirit
N. James
O. Jesus
P. John
Q. John the Baptist
R. Joseph and Mary
S. Judas Maccabeus
T. Luke
U. Mattathias
V. Matthew
W. Mark
X. Nero
Y. Pastoral Letters
Z. Paul
AA. Pauline Epistles
AB. Pax Romana
AC. Peter
AD. Pharisees
AE. Philip

ANSWER KEY

26. __N__ leader in the church in Jerusalem
27. __D__ town in which Jesus was born
28. __L__ Roman governor of Judea at the time of Jesus' birth
29. __V__ tax collector who became a disciple
30. __AJ__ recipient of Luke's two-volume work
31. __Y__ letters of instruction and guidance for leaders
32. __J__ Jewish group that resisted Hellenization; "pious ones"
33. __U__ elderly priest who led revolt against Syria
34. __M__ given by Jesus when he ascended
35. __AG__ letters written while Paul was under house arrest
36. __S__ recaptured the temple from the Seleucids
37. __AI__ Gospels that have similar content and style

AF. Pompey
AG. Prison Letters
AH. Stephen
AI. Synoptic Gospels
AJ. Theophilus
AK. turning water to wine

List: Complete each list. (1 pt. each)

The 3 types of addressees for the epistles:

1. a particular church
2. a group of churches
3. an individual person

The three sections of an epistle:

1. Opening/ Greeting
2. Body
3. Closing

Books Containing Apocalyptic Literature:

1. Daniel
2. Ezekiel
3. Revelation

The Prison Letters:

1. Ephesians
2. Philippians
3. Colossians
4. Philemon

The Pastoral Letters:

1. I Timothy
2. II Timothy
3. Titus

Short Answer: Write the answer that best completes the sentence. (1 pt.)

The disciples became witnesses to __Jerusalem, Judea and Samaria, and all the earth__

Vocabulary: Choose the answer that best fits the definition. (1 pt. each)

1. X a sacrifice that bears God's wrath
2. J a person who is not Jewish
3. AC study of God
4. F the study of the last things
5. C chosen Messiah
6. N the spreading of the Greek culture and way of life
7. H trust in God and his promises
8. AD a person who testifies to events or facts within his own knowledge
9. R made right with God
10. I readiness and willingness to give
11. T the Roman name for Canaan
12. W persistence in spite of difficulties
13. O false teaching
14. U Jesus' method of teaching using stories
15. S one who chooses to suffer death rather than renounce his religious beliefs
16. Q inward hope despite circumstances
17. E separation because of different opinions
18. A a revelation of hidden realities given by God
19. Z deliverance from the power and penalty of sin
20. Y to make a friend of an enemy
21. V torturing or killing people because of their beliefs
22. D spread of Jews all over the Roman Empire
23. B an official messenger of the gospel
24. L ancient belief that considered all matter to be evil and only the spiritual to be good
25. AA language that uses images instead of direct expression
26. AE God's anger and judgment towards sin
27. AB local place of worship for Jews during the diaspora
28. G ground for belief or disbelief; proof
29. M unearned favor and love of God
30. K the good news of the salvation provided by Jesus' life, death, and resurrection
31. P considering others more important than yourself

A. apocalypse
B. apostle
C. Christ
D. diaspora
E. division
F. eschatology
G. evidence
H. faith
I. generosity
J. Gentile
K. gospel
L. Gnosticism
M. grace
N. Hellenization
O. heresy
P. humility
Q. joy
R. justification
S. martyr
T. Palestine
U. parable
V. persecution
W. perseverance
X. propitiation
Y. reconciliation
Z. salvation
AA. symbolism
AB. synagogue
AC. theology
AD. witness
AE. wrath

Scripture: Write each verse from memory. Be accurate. (5 pts. each)

I Corinthians 13:4-8 Love suffereth long, and is kind; love envieth not; love vaunteth not itself, is not puffed up, doth not behave itself unseemly, seeketh not her own, is not easily provoked, thinketh no evil; rejoiceth not in iniquity, but rejoiceth in truth; beareth all things, believeth all things, hopeth all things, endureth all things. Love never faileth

Ephesians 2:8-9 For by grace are ye saved through faith; and that not of yourselves: it is the gift of God: Not of works, lest any man should boast.

II Timothy 3:16-17 All scripture is given by inspiration of God, and is profitable for doctrine, for reproof, for correction, for instruction in righteousness: That the man of God may be perfect, thoroughly furnished unto all good works.

Extra Credit: Write each verse from memory (5 pts. each)

Mark 8:34-37 Whosoever will come after me, let him deny himself and take up his cross and follow me. For whosoever will save his life shall lose it; but whosoever shall lose his life for my sake and the gospel's, the same shall save it. For what shall it profit a man, if he shall gain the whole world, and lose his own soul? Or what shall a man give in exchange for his soul?

Revelation 21:3-4 And I heard a great voice out of heaven saying, Behold, the tabernacle of God is with men, and he will dwell with them, and they shall be his people, and God himself shall be with them, and be their God. And God shall wipe away all tears from their eyes; and there shall be no more death, neither sorrow, nor crying, neither shall there be any more pain: for the former things are passed away.